Youth Involvement in the Child Welfare and Juvenile Justice Systems

A CASE OF DOUBLE JEOPARDY?

Leslee Morris
and Madelyn Freundlich

CWLA Press
Washington, DC

CWLA Press is an imprint of the Child Welfare League of America. The Child Welfare League of America is the nation's oldest and largest membership-based child welfare organization. We are committed to engaging people everywhere in promoting the well-being of children, youth, and their families, and protecting every child from harm. Proceeds from the sale of this book benefit CWLA's programs in behalf of children and families.

CHILD WELFARE LEAGUE OF AMERICA, INC.
HEADQUARTERS
440 First Street, NW, Third Floor, Washington, DC 20001-2085
E-mail: books@cwla.org
www.cwla.org

CURRENT PRINTING (last digit)
10 9 8 7 6 5 4 3 2 1

Cover and text design by Jennifer Geanakos
Edited by Julie Gwin
Printed in the United States of America

ISBN 1-58760-025-0

Library of Congress Cataloging-in-Publication Data
Morris, Leslee.
Youth involvement in the child welfare and juvenile justice systems : a case of double jeopardy? / Leslee Morris and Madelyn Freundlich.
    p. cm.
ISBN 1-58760-025-0 (alk. paper)
1. Child welfare--United States. 2. Juvenile delinquency--United States.
3. Juvenile justice, Administration of--United States. I. Freundlich, Madelyn.
II. Title.

HV741.M67 2004
364.36'0973--dc22   2004017667

Contents

PART III

Acknowledgments

Children's Rights acknowledges the support of the Overbrook Foundation, whose generous contribution made this project possible. Children's Rights thanks Nicole Biguenet, Cara Chambers, and Sabra Gandhi, associates at Cleary, Gottlieb, Steen & Hamilton, for their significant contributions of their legal talents and insights. We also extend our appreciation to Jessica Heldman and Jana Bockstein, who contributed greatly to the report. We are grateful to Dr. Mary Ann Jones for her tireless assistance with the design of the project, her important contributions to the work, and her always thoughtful and purposeful review of the report. Appreciation also is extended to Carmen Hernandez, Policy Assistant, for contributing her administrative expertise to the development and production of the report.

Finally, we extend our deepest appreciation to the youth, foster parents, judges, and other professionals who agreed to be resources for this project and who spoke with us frankly about these important matters.

PART I

Introduction

Imagine that you are a 14-year-old. You have been living in a group home for the past nine months, after being removed from your parent's care due to neglect, and you have been committed to the local department of social services. One evening on your way to the group home, you are picked up by the police in your community for getting into a fight, and they charge you with assault. You are scheduled to appear in court tomorrow for adjudication. You are weighed down with questions: Who will come to court with you? Will anyone speak in court on your behalf? Will your child welfare caseworker be at the hearing? How will the judge view you? Where will you go from there? Whom do you turn to with questions?

Little is known about what occurs when youth in foster care are arrested and brought before the juvenile court on delinquency petitions. Although some professionals have recognized the need to address issues affecting youth who find themselves in the overlap of the child welfare and juvenile justice systems, researchers have made no systematic effort to examine the experiences of these youth or the outcomes for them. Because these issues have not been studied to any meaningful extent, little is known about how young people fare when they find themselves involved in both the child welfare and the juvenile justice systems, the extent to which foster parents and child welfare agency staff serve as advocates for youth who appear before the juvenile court on delinquency charges, or the approaches used by courts to address the complex issues presented when a young person in foster care is charged with a delinquent act.

Previous research suggests that the outcomes for these youth may be particularly poor. Based on what is known about the relationship between child maltreatment and subsequent involvement with the juvenile justice and criminal justice systems, it is clear that young people in foster care are at particular risk of engaging in conduct that will bring them into contact with the justice system. At the same time, it is cause for concern that youth in foster care who are charged with delinquent acts may lack the very supports that will lead to more positive outcomes, such as the use of social service alternatives, as opposed to institutional confinement.

Moreover, it may be anticipated that for youth in foster care, the possibility of involvement by a responsible adult—their birthparents, their foster parents, or the caseworkers who represent the agency holding legal custody of the youth—may be unlikely. Whereas birthparents of youth who are not in foster care may advocate on behalf of their children when they become involved with the juvenile justice system, birthparents who have lost custody of their children, or nonrelated adults such as foster parents or caseworkers, may not press the court to allow them to participate. Foster parents, for example, may not see their role as extending to advocacy with the juvenile court on behalf of a child in their care. At the same time, foster parents do not have the legal standing of birthparents, and when they do attempt to advocate on behalf of a child in their care, juvenile courts may perceive them more as temporary caregivers than as important parental figures in youths' lives. Child welfare caseworkers may be uncertain of their roles in relation to juvenile justice proceedings, and they may have their own biases regarding the wisdom of involving foster parents in juvenile court proceedings.

Questions abound about the experiences of youth in foster care who are brought before the juvenile court on delinquency charges: Is their involvement with the juvenile justice system the result of their independent actions leading to an arrest, or is it precipitated by the child welfare system itself (for example, when a foster parent is the complaining witness or a group facility summons the police regarding a resident)? How do juvenile court judges assess the youth's situation when he or she is already in foster care? What influences judicial decisions for youth who already have been adjudicated as dependent? To what extent does the presence of a birthparent or parent substitute (such as a foster parent or child welfare caseworker) influence judicial decisions about disposition alternatives?

Other issues relate to the factors that promote or work against the involvement of interested adults on behalf of youth in foster care charged with delinquency offenses. For example, do youths' caseworkers and foster parents receive formal written notice of the charges against the young person? Are these adults likely to appear on behalf of the youth at various hearings, such as preliminary hearings, arraignments, adjudications, and disposition hearings? Are any factors associated with their willingness to appear, such as the nature of the charge, the age of the young person, how long the child has been in their care, or the quality of the relationship between the young person and the adult? If caseworkers or foster parents are notified and appear before the court, are these adults given an opportunity to be heard? Has practice been affected by the new federal requirements under the Adoption and Safe Families Act of 1997 (ASFA, P.L. 105-193) regarding the rights of foster parents, relative caregivers, and prospective adoptive parents to be given notice and an opportunity to be heard at legal proceedings involving children in their care? To what extent do foster parents believe that their viewpoints inform courts' decisions regarding disposition outcomes for youth?

Finally, of particular importance are the perspectives of young people who find themselves in the overlap of the two systems. How do youth view their foster care status when confronted with delinquency charges? Do they wish to have interested adults with them when they appear in juvenile court? If so, which adults are most important to them? When faced with an involvement with both systems, what do youth want to see happen—a return to foster care or some other option that takes them out of the child welfare system?

This study was designed to answer these questions. The study provides an account of the experiences of young people in foster care who became involved with the juvenile justice system as a result of a delinquent act, the views of foster parents concerning their role when youth in their care are arrested, the perspectives of juvenile court judges regarding these youth, and the perceptions of child welfare agencies concerning their role when children in foster care face delinquency charges. In addition, this study identifies innovative programs that planners have developed to address the issues affecting children and youth in the overlap of the child welfare and juvenile justice systems. It also examines the extent to which law, policy, and practice support appropriate outcomes for young people in foster care with subsequent involvement in delinquency. Furthermore, it explores the extent to which child welfare agencies and foster parents are able to and actually do advocate on behalf of these young people. Based on the results of this research, the authors recommend improvements in both child welfare and juvenile justice practice and policy, with the goal of improving the response of the systems to youth in foster care who commit delinquent acts.

Literature Review

The research literature establishes a relationship between childhood maltreatment and delinquent behavior. Numerous studies indicate that victims of childhood abuse and neglect are at an increased risk of delinquent behavior, although maltreatment is not determinative of delinquency (English, Widom, & Brandford, 2001; Maxfield & Widom, 1996; Pawaserat, 1991; Smith & Thornberry, 1995; Widom, 1989). Several of these studies also have addressed the relationship between foster care and delinquency, and placement instability and delinquency. The research is quite limited regarding how youth fare in the juvenile justice system and the quality of the collaboration between the child welfare and juvenile justice systems.

Most research in this area samples maltreated children and follows them to determine rates of subsequent criminal behavior. Despite the fact that the studies employ a variety of methods, focus on different age groups, and use differing definitions of *maltreatment* and *delinquency*, the research strongly suggests that maltreated youth are significantly more likely to become involved in delinquent behavior than their nonmaltreated peers.

- In a series of studies (Maxfield & Widom, 1996; Widom, 1989, 1992), researchers followed 908 children in the Midwest who were abused or neglected through their teen years and into adulthood through an examination of official criminal records. The researchers compared them with a matched control group of 667 children of the same age, gender, race, and social class. The researchers found that childhood abuse and neglect increased the likelihood of arrest as a juvenile by 59%. The abused and neglected group differed from the control group in several key areas: They were arrested more frequently, committed nearly twice as many offenses, and were younger at the time of their first arrest.

- A study by Smith and Thornberry (1995) confirmed a significant relationship between child maltreatment and both self-reported delinquency and official delinquency for youth in upstate New York. The researchers found that the maltreated youth were significantly more likely than the nonmaltreated group to have an official record of delinquency (45% vs. 32%) or a self-report of delinquent behavior (79% vs. 70%). The results also suggested that more extreme forms of maltreatment are related to higher rates of delinquency.

- A study by English et al. (2001) that replicated and extended Widom's original study on the cycle of violence (1992) found that abused and neglected children were 4.8 times more likely than a matched control group of nonmaltreated youth to be arrested as juveniles. In addition, abused and neglected youth were 11 times more likely to be arrested for a violent crime as a juvenile than were their nonmaltreated counterparts.

- Using a retrospective design (in contrast to the previous studies), a 1991 study by Pawaserat focused on court-referred juvenile offenders in Milwaukee County, Wisconsin, to determine the prevalence of child maltreatment histories among that population. It revealed that 66% of male offenders and 39% of female offenders had been victims in substantiated reports of maltreatment.

Other research suggests that placement in foster care is associated with subsequent delinquency.

- In New York City, an Armstrong (1998) study examined the flow of adolescents into the Administration for Children's Services (ACS), New York City's child welfare agency, through other government systems. ACS staff initially believed that many adolescents entered ACS care through the juvenile justice system, however, the analysis revealed that the majority of the adolescents received from the juvenile justice system were actually being returned to ACS after having been in ACS custody initially and then entering the juvenile justice system. Most of the adolescents had been in the care of ACS at the time of their arrest. The researchers also found that 15% of the youth in two New York City detention facilities were in the child welfare system when they entered detention, a rate eight times what was expected based on census data.

- A study by Ryan and Testa (2004) established that the rate of delinquency increases among those removed from their homes and placed in foster care. The researchers found that substantiated victims of maltreatment average 47% higher delinquency rates compared with children not indicated for abuse or neglect. Moreover, 16% of children placed in foster care experienced at least one delinquency petition compared with 9% of all maltreatment victims who were not removed from their families. The researchers found that for girls, placement into foster homes—even if stable—is highly correlated with delinquency. For boys, however, placement instability, rather than placement itself, increased the risk of delinquency.

- A study by Jonson-Reid and Barth (2003) examined school-age children who entered out-of-home placement supervised by probation departments after they left child welfare foster care. The researchers found that instability in child welfare placements significantly increased the risk of transition to foster care supervised by probation departments. Another study by Jonson-Reid and Barth (2000) involved a prospective examination of adolescent incarceration for serious felony offenses and other violent offenses as a postdischarge outcome for children in out-of-home placements. The researchers found that children with multiple placements had a higher risk of incarceration for a serious or violent offense during adolescence. Specifically, girls with prior child welfare foster care spells had a rate of entry into the California Youth Authority (CYA), the statewide system housing serious youthful offenders, that was 10 times higher than females in the general population. Males with prior child welfare placements had entry rates into CYA that were five times higher than males in the general population. Moreover, the research revealed that among children with two spells in foster care, the rate of entry into CYA was about 10 per 1,000, but among children with three spells, the entry rate rose to about 30 per 1,000.

- Another study (Runyan & Gould, 1985) found that among children in foster care, an increase in the number of foster home placements correlated with increased numbers of delinquency convictions.

- During the course of a recent study in Arizona, the National Center for Juvenile Justice (NCJJ) obtained a preliminary estimate of the number of dual-system youth in that state's two most-populous counties. Specifically, in the summer of 2003, NCJJ contacted the juvenile probation departments in Maricopa County (the Phoenix metropolitan area) and Pima County (the Tucson metropolitan area) to obtain initial estimates of the numbers of juvenile probationers who were also involved in active dependency cases (i.e., the number of probationers with an active dependency petition or an open dependency case occurring at any time during the probation period). Officials in Maricopa County reported that slightly less than 5,000 juveniles were on probation in June 2003 and estimated that 500 to 600 of these were dual-jurisdiction cases. Pima County officials reported 1,400 juvenile probationers at the time of NCJJ's contact and estimated that 140 to 170 of these were also at some stage of active dependency. In other words, in June 2003, there were between 640 and 770 dual-system cases, representing 10% to 12% of juvenile probationers in Arizona's two most-populous jurisdictions (Gene Siegel, personal communication, January 22, 2004).[1]

- Research conducted by the Vera Institute (Armstrong, 1998) indicated that in New York City, youth in foster care were significantly more likely to be arrested at home than were nonfoster youth: 4% of non-ACS youth were arrested at their homes, 36% of youth in foster care were arrested at their foster homes, and 55% of youth in congregate care were arrested at their placements. The study found that almost half of the teenagers in a group home in New York City had been arrested as a result of an incident in placement.

- In a series of studies, researchers found little difference between the arrest records of abused and neglected youngsters who remained at home and those who were placed outside the home due to abuse and neglect (Maxfield & Widom, 1996; Widom, 1989, 1992). Children who were moved three or more times while in out-of-home care, however, had significantly higher juvenile arrest rates (almost twice as high) than children who were moved fewer than three times, suggesting the importance of placement stability.

- English et al. (2001) concluded that abused and neglected children removed from parental custody and placed in nonrelative foster care were significantly more likely to be arrested for a juvenile crime than youth living with their primary caregivers, relatives, or kin.

The research literature has focused only to a limited extent on how youth in foster care fare in the juvenile justice system.

- A study conducted by the Vera Institute (Conger & Ross, 2001) quantified a foster care bias in detention decisions in New York City. The researchers found that children in foster care who commit delinquent acts are more likely than other youth who commit similar crimes to be sent to juvenile detention to await trial. Specifically, the research revealed that the probability of detention for youth in foster care charged with misdemeanors and minor felonies was 10 percentage points higher than the probability for youth not in foster care, controlling for other influences.

- A study by the American Bar Association Center on Children and the Law (Davies & Davidson, 2001) examined the effect of parental involvement on delinquency proceedings and found that outcomes for youth charged with delinquency offenses are more positive when their parents are involved with the juvenile justice system on behalf of their children. Importantly, the researchers found that the courts generally did not actively engage with birthparents, who often felt that they received insufficient support, education, and respect from the juvenile justice system. Among the reasons found for the limited parental involvement was that the juvenile had been in state custody for a significant period of time and the parents assumed their attendance would not have an effect on the proceedings.

- In connection with adult involvement on behalf of youth in the juvenile justice system, Deihl, Martin, and Nunez (2002) examined how training caregivers in the child welfare system affects caregiver participation in dependency court hearings. The researchers found that participation in training increased the likelihood that caregivers attended court.

The research literature has focused to a limited extent on the ability of the child welfare and juvenile systems to act collaboratively on behalf of youth who are involved with both systems.

- A study by the Vera Institute (Armstrong, 1998) found a lack of mutual understanding and cooperation among the child welfare, juvenile justice, mental health, and status-offender systems in New York City, resulting in duplication of services, unnecessary transaction costs, and poor results for youth. The study made several recommendations to improve interagency cooperation and reduce the unnecessary movement of adolescents between government systems.

- The Child Welfare League of America (2002), in a survey of 228 juvenile justice probation supervisors, court administrators, and directors of court service units representing 42 states, found that nearly 9 in 10 responding agencies did not have a program designed to serve juvenile offenders who had been identified as previous victims of maltreatment. Only one in three agencies indicated that information documenting a history of maltreatment was reported at the entry point to the juvenile justice system, the arrest report. Approximately three of four juvenile justice agencies had policies, procedures, or regulations supporting collaboration with child welfare agencies who had custody of juvenile offenders with histories of maltreatment. These efforts included multidisciplinary teams, memorandums of understanding, informal agreements, mandatory reporting to the custodial agency, and dual responsibility for youth with juvenile delinquency and dependency court involvement.

The Study's Method

This study involved three research methods: qualitative research using in-depth individual and focus group interviews, research into programmatic approaches that meet the needs of youth involved in both the child welfare and juvenile justice systems, and legal research regarding the rights of foster parents and other interested parties when youth in foster care appear in delinquency court.

Qualitative Research

A qualitative approach using interviews with key stakeholders afforded an opportunity to obtain insight into the firsthand experiences of youth in foster care who were arrested for delinquent acts and of other key players responsible for this population of youth. The researchers interviewed the following groups using preset protocols:

- **Nationally recognized professionals with backgrounds in child welfare, juvenile justice, or both fields.** Based on information gleaned from the research literature review and from their own familiarity with the relevant fields, the researchers identified five seasoned professionals with backgrounds in child welfare, juvenile justice, or both fields to assist in providing a "lay of the land" view regarding children in foster care who appear in court on delinquency charges. The researchers contacted these individuals, representing four states, by letter to explain the goals of the study and to invite the recipient to participate in a discussion to identify the issues of importance when youth in foster care are brought before the juvenile court on delinquency petitions. The researchers contacted each professional by telephone to arrange a phone interview. All five invited professionals participated in individual conversations. The information obtained through these conversations helped shape the subsequent research.

- **Young adults who had lived with a foster family or in group care and were arrested for committing delinquent acts while in care.** Working with New York City–based youth advocacy groups including Voices of Youth, the researchers identified 12 young adults who formerly had lived in foster care when arrested on one or more delinquency charges. They interviewed these young adults individually or in small groups. Each interview lasted between one and one and a half hours. Each participating youth had lived with a foster family or in group care and had been arrested on one or more delinquency charges while in care. The young adults ranged in age from 18 to 22 years, with the exception of one young adult who was in his 30s. There were nine male and three female interviewees. All interviewees were either African American or Latino. The researchers also gave the young adults the opportunity to complete a written survey to provide any information they chose not to discuss during the interviews.

- **Foster parents who had been or currently are a foster parent for a youth who was arrested for committing a delinquent act.** Foster parents who were in attendance at the National Foster Parent Association 2003 annual conference in Des Moines, Iowa, received a flyer explaining the project and an invitation to attend a one-hour focus group. Eighteen individuals reported to the focus group; one was rejected as not having relevant experience. Fourteen women and three men participated. Two married couples were among the 17 participants. The group was fairly evenly divided between white foster parents (nine) and foster parents of color (eight). Although the researchers did not ask the foster parents to provide their ages, most of the foster parents appeared to be 50 years of age or older. Only one foster parent appeared to be in her 30s. The foster parents participating in the focus group represented six different states: California, Colorado, Illinois, Iowa, Louisiana, and Minnesota. The researchers conducted the focus group in accordance with a preset focus group protocol. The researchers made follow-up telephone calls to two foster parents to solicit further information on points raised during the focus group. They also gave participants the opportunity to complete a written survey to provide any information they chose not to discuss during the focus group.

* **Juvenile court judges.** The researchers used their communication with child welfare and juvenile justice professionals to generate a list of juvenile court judges with significant experience with both the child welfare and juvenile justice systems. They contacted 15 judges whose courts were located in various parts of the country by letter to explain the goals of the study and invite the judge to participate in an interview. They also contacted each judge by telephone to arrange an interview. Ten judges in nine different states completed the interview, either by telephone or in person.

* **Public child welfare administrators.** Working in conjunction with the National Association of Public Child Welfare Administrators, the researchers identified five public child welfare administrators with significant experience with the juvenile justice system. The researchers contacted each administrator by letter to explain the goals of the study and invite the administrator to participate in an interview. They also contacted each administrator by telephone to arrange an interview. All five administrators completed the interview by telephone. Interviews lasted between 30 and 60 minutes. In two instances, child welfare administrators met with child welfare caseworkers prior to the interview to gather information. In two cases, juvenile justice administrators also participated in the interviews.

Identification of Innovative Programs

The researchers undertook a review of child welfare and juvenile justice publications to identify existing programs that respond to the population of youth involved in the child welfare and juvenile justice systems. They consulted the following sources as part of the research:

- the World Wide Web;

- bound volumes of publications, including the *Juvenile and Family Court Journal*, the *Journal of Juvenile Law*, and *Child Welfare*;

- the LegalTrac database, which allows searches of all legal periodicals by subject, keyword, and other advanced search options; and

- the EBSCO Host Research Database, which allows searches of thousands of periodicals related to the social sciences, searchable by subject, journal issue, or author.

Legal Research

The authors conducted legal research into the statutes of 16 states[2] and the District of Columbia to determine the extent to which the law requires notification of child welfare agencies and foster parents when youth in foster care are arrested, brought to a juvenile detention or intake facility, and brought before the juvenile court on delinquency petitions. They identified statues that grant foster parents rights concerning youth in care who are arrested. The researchers contacted stakeholders in eight of the states by telephone to gather information about actual practice in those states.

Method Limitations

The study has certain limitations that must be recognized. Its reliance on qualitative methods provides an in-depth understanding of the issues from the perspectives of the stakeholders who were interviewed, but does not permit generalization to all individuals in the stakeholder groups. In addition, the small number of participants who were interviewed in each stakeholder group limits the generalizability of the findings. Finally, the study's reliance on self-reporting poses limitations on the data. This study, however, adds significantly to the very limited knowledge base on youth in foster care who become involved in the juvenile justice system. It provides important insights into the experiences of and outcomes for youth involved in the child welfare and juvenile justice systems from multiple perspectives. Its inclusion of young adults with direct experience with both systems is a particularly strong feature of this study. The inclusion of legal research and research into programs that address the needs of this population of youth further strengthens the contributions of this study. Despite its limitations, this study provides useful information about the issues on which future qualitative and quantitative research should focus.

PART II

The Results

The results of this study are organized into three sections. The first section reports the results from interviews with different stakeholder groups. In the second section, the authors present information on innovative programs that attempt to respond to youth who are dually involved in the child welfare and juvenile justice systems. In the third section, they present the results of legal research into the statutory rights of foster parents or other relevant parties when youth in care face delinquency charges.

Interview and Focus Group Results

The following chapters include a summary of interviews with five nationally recognized professionals who are leaders in child welfare, juvenile justice, or both fields. The researchers consulted these individuals to obtain a foundational understanding of issues regarding the population of youth who become involved in the juvenile justice system while in foster care. Next, the authors present results of interviews with two groups: young adults who were formerly in foster care and foster parents. Finally, they present the findings of interviews with juvenile court judges and child welfare administrators.

Innovative Programs

The second section of Part II examines programs in nine states that link services for youth who are involved in both the child welfare and juvenile justice systems. These innovative new efforts blend funding streams, provide cross-over case management, and have implemented such court models as one family–one judge, to better serve youth in need.

Current Law

The final part of this study examined legal mandates that require courts and agencies to notify significant adults in the lives of children and youth in foster care when these youth are arrested and charged with a delinquent act. The analysis includes a study of both federal requirements and the legal statutes of 16 states and the District of Columbia.

Interviews with Child Welfare and Juvenile Justice Professionals

Five seasoned professionals with experience in child welfare, juvenile justice, or both fields gave their insight into the issues of importance when youth in foster care face delinquency charges. Their impressions helped refine the study's research focus. The comments of these professionals fell into four topics:

- how foster care may contribute to juvenile delinquency,

- how judges may perceive youth in foster care,

- the functioning of child welfare and juvenile justice systems, and

- the needs of this population of youth.

How Foster Care May Contribute to Juvenile Delinquency

These informants agreed that it is little surprise that many adolescents in foster care commit delinquent acts. They commented that youth who spend their lives being moved from place to place infrequently develop trusting relationships, and the commission of crimes is an outgrowth of the distrust and anger they develop. Informants generally agreed that "we reap what we sow" regarding this population of youth. To that end, they emphasized the need for a greater commitment to finding permanent homes for children more expeditiously than is the case currently.

This group of informants expressed concern about the speed with which youth in foster care are reported to the police for what might be behavior problems common in adolescents regardless of living situation. For example, they noted that often, child welfare agencies handle youth in care with a very heavy hand and readily contact the police or prosecutor for problems that could be dealt with internally. These professionals noted that it is important to consider the underlying circumstances when a youth in care is charged with a delinquent act, particularly whether the agency's practice contributed to the arrest or charge. They felt it is important to look at the facts in any individual case to determine whether the youth actually belongs in delinquency court or found himself or herself in court because child welfare staff wanted to "wash their hands" of the youth. Similarly, informants were concerned that both group home staff and foster parents may unnecessarily summon the police when a youth's behavior becomes unruly.

How Judges May Perceive Youth in Foster Care

These professionals also expressed concern about judges' possible perceptions of youth in foster care. They agreed that when a youth appears in delinquency court without family present, a judge may be inclined to think the young person has no support and may believe that the only way to secure the youth is to confine him or her. They also were concerned that judges tend to refer youth for services without much information about the nature or purpose of those services. The professionals were concerned that judges who are not well informed about referred services may be setting youth up for failure.

The Functioning of Child Welfare and Juvenile Justice Systems

These professionals were concerned about the confusion that occurs when a child welfare agency loses physical custody of a youth but retains legal custody—a likely situation when a youth in care is arrested and detained. Because the child welfare agency retains legal custody, it continues to have planning responsibility for the child, but these professionals believed that the agency often simply declines to continue working with the youth.

A related concern is the tendency of both child welfare and juvenile justice systems to push youth into the other system when a question arises as to which agency is responsible for the youth. This group of informants asserted that each system may press for the youth's transfer to the other system so that financial responsibility for the youth also will transfer.

These professionals were concerned about poor communication between juvenile justice systems and child welfare agencies. Two of the five informants stated that agency representatives or group home staff members usually attend delinquency court proceedings with youth when they receive timely notice of the proceedings, but that all too often they do not receive this notice and thus, do not appear.

These informants emphasized the need for jurisdictions to develop mechanisms to improve coordination between juvenile justice workers and child welfare workers. In one informant's system, child welfare and juvenile justice workers meet every six weeks for several hours to make policy decisions. Another informant commented her county created a position specifically designed to facilitate system interaction several years ago. The same informant stated that her jurisdiction developed a memorandum of agreement stating that the child welfare agency is always the lead agency when a youth in care is charged with delinquency, but that child welfare staff act in consultation with the youth's probation officer.

All informants mentioned the need for cross-training of child welfare and juvenile justice staff. Three informants also mentioned the utility of having one "pot of money" available to both child welfare and juvenile justice departments so agencies feel less tension about which system has financial responsibility for the youth.

The Needs of This Population of Youth

The group of professionals expressed particular concerns about youth in foster care who have been freed for adoption and subsequently appear in court on delinquency charges. They emphasized the importance of directing effort and attention toward preserving the youth's relationships with prospective adoptive families. One informant, for example, stated that those families need to be "fortified" through support groups and other resources.

They also contended that agencies must pay greater attention to the mental health and special education needs of youth in foster care to prevent them from moving into the juvenile justice system. Moreover, informants noted a significant need for better assessment of and response to such needs when youth enter the juvenile justice system. One professional reported that high numbers of illiterate teenagers arrive at detention centers without previously having been identified as having learning problems.

Young Adult
Interviews

▬ ▬

The researchers interviewed 12 young adults with histories of involvement with both the child welfare and juvenile justice systems. The majority of the young adults (nine) had lived in both foster family homes and group homes. Two had lived only in group homes; one had lived only with a foster family.

Of the 11 young adults who had lived in a group home, 7 were arrested while living in the group home, 1 was arrested while absent without leave (AWOL) from the group home, and 3 were arrested either before or after group home care. Of the 10 youth who had lived with a foster family, 6 were arrested while living with the family and 4 were arrested while in other living arrangements.

The most common offenses police charged the young adults with were assault and drug-related charges. Other charges included shoplifting, trespassing, burglary, and metro card (public transportation) violations. The researchers asked the young adults about their experiences with the juvenile justice system. Their comments focused on the following areas:

- judges' awareness of foster care status and young adults' perceptions of how foster care status affected court proceedings;

- how young adults' experiences in foster care affected their attitudes toward committing crimes;

- police intervention in group homes;

- the group home environment;

- experiences with foster families;

- who, if anyone, attended court appearances with youth, and young adults' perceptions of how the presence or absence of an adult affected court proceedings;

- young adults' experiences in jail; and

- legal representation.

In addition, the participants made recommendations to improve outcomes for youth who are involved in both the foster care and juvenile justice systems.

Judges' and Young Adults' Perceptions of Foster Care Status

Each of the young adults appeared before a judge on at least one charge, and some appeared on more than one charge. In most cases, young adults felt that the judges knew they were in foster care. Of the young adults who felt that the judge was aware of their foster care status, most agreed that the judge received that information in written form.

Three young adults stated that for at least one of their appearances, the judge was unaware that they were in foster care. One young woman who appeared on a metro card violation stated, "The judge didn't ask [whether I was in foster care]. It was a quick proceeding, and he didn't even ask my name."

In some instances, young adults felt that the fact they were in foster care had a negative effect on the way the judge perceived them. Young people stated:

The judge knew I was in foster care because he read the report. I think it must have worked against me—he thought I was a bad person—like, why is this man in care? He must have done something wrong to end up in care.

It looks like, well, she's in a foster home, she's gotta be guilty. We get looked at different. Like there's something wrong with us because we're in foster care. Sometimes they treat you harder, it depends on the judge.

In other instances, young adults felt that the fact that they were in foster care had a mitigating effect. One young man felt that his background as a youth in care helped him in court: "My history, my family history of drug abuse helped me get out." Another young adult stated, "I don't think we get treated worse. If anything, we probably get treated a little better—more leniently." One young man stated that the judge commented on his background in court:

The judge said, "You're a lucky child. I am [giving you this sentence] today only due to your background, your history, your life, and what's been happening to you all your life. We know you've been in the system since you were five...that's the only reason I am doing this today."

How Experiences in Foster Care Affected Young Adults' Attitudes Toward Crime

Young adults generally agreed that their experiences in foster care contributed to what they described as their anger and indifference to others. One young adult who had lived in both a foster home and a group home stated:

If kids lived with their family, maybe they'd try not to get in trouble. But they don't have a family—so what if their group home or foster family finds out—they're not the real parents. You figure you got nothing to lose because you're not with your family.

Another young adult who also lived in both a foster home and a group home said, "I started a lot of fights. I didn't have a family so to me it was nothing—there ain't nothing to life, I ain't got a family." A young woman who lived with a foster family and in group care stated, "Nobody shows you respect so you don't show them respect—you lash out at everybody...nobody liked me, so I'd just fight." A young man remarked that his experience living in a group home led him to join a gang. "Being in a group home is one of the main reasons why I think I went into a gang—I always wanted a family bond and at the time I saw it as a family."

Police Intervention in Group Homes

In some situations, police arrested youth living in group homes for incidents that occurred in the group homes. The youth stated that favoritism, stealing, and inattentiveness by staff were commonplace in group homes and often led to fights and the police being summoned to the group home. One young man who was arrested for fighting in a group home said, "Sometimes I got [treated favorably by staff]...and two people jumped me." Another young man who was arrested for cutting a peer in the group home with a knife stated that he was bullied by that individual and cut the bully to make him stop.

Young adults stated that staff often called the police as a first resort when fighting occurred in a group home. One young adult who was arrested for fighting in a group home said, "The staff are quick to call the cops—to get you off their hands." A young woman commented, "They call the cops all the time for fighting in the group home—that's normal. Youth are always getting sent to jail for a fight that could have been avoided." One young adult stated, "Some places are very low tolerance...but most places have some type of regulatory process before they call the police."

Another young adult disagreed, saying, "It's supposed to be a process [before they call the police] but the staff panics—they're so used to reacting that way." Another young man commented that the security guards who were in his group home were physically out of shape and hesitant to intervene when fights occurred: "If a fight happens, they run." Two young adults stated that the group home staff should be able to handle fights internally and should call the police only "when it gets to weapons."

Young adults generally agreed that, over time, group home staff began to take incidents in group homes—including fighting—more seriously and that group home staff were more likely to call the police. One young man observed, "There was a time when kids would steal petty cash and it was nothing and they'd handle it internally, and now it's grand larceny—'You're going to jail.' Youth used to be handled internally, even for serious crimes—now they prosecute you."

Only one young adult stated that the group home staff hesitated before calling the police for incidents in the group home. The young adult, who lived in a group home for people with mental illnesses stated, "The workers would try to work out the situation and try to avoid calling the police."

The Group Home Environment

Most of the young adults who experienced group home life complained adamantly about conditions in group homes, including abuse by staff, staff's lack of guidance or compassion, and problems associated with sharing living space with other youth who were difficult to live with or who had been placed in the group home because they committed crimes. Interviewees stated that agencies often circulate youth who live in group homes and display problematic behaviors to other group homes instead of giving them treatment or attention. Young adults commented that they themselves were returned to the same group home after being arrested for problems that arose in that group home.

One young man, who was arrested while AWOL from his group home, stated, "I would rather be in jail than the group home." A young adult who was arrested for participating in a riot in his group home stated:

I learned in a group home how to be in prison—how to beat the rap—group home is where you learn the tricks of the trade, to master it. It's the West Point of crime, it's like pre-prison camp.

A young adult who was arrested for possession of drugs and attempt to sell drugs stated, "Kids in the group home sold drugs, so that's [how I started selling drugs too.]"

Another young man stated that he frequently was out on the street because "the staff were assholes so I was hardly ever there." He said:

A lot of kids [from group homes] get into trouble because there's no guidance there...they don't ask you how you did in school today, if you did your homework. The staff is abusive, they talk down to you, make you do [stuff] you don't want to do, you're mixed in there with people you don't like, it smells there, the food is shitty...a group home ain't nothing but a place to sleep. It shouldn't be called "home," it should be called "group house." It was nothing like a home, it was like a jail.

This young man was involved in a fight between two gangs in which he was shot and stabbed. He stated that the group home staff "didn't know I had been shot or stabbed when I came back from the hospital—they never really paid me any attention." The young man reported that the group home staff learned about the gang fight only when the police appeared at the group home two weeks later to arrest him.

One young adult, speaking of group home staff members, stated:

[Youth] ask for something to eat or a bar of soap, and they say no because they're too lazy to get it for us or because they're busy talking to each other. When they come to work, they're supposed to be working with us. When we don't get the attention we're supposed to, we get upset [and fights occur]...You have staff that when they get upset they punch holes in the walls and flip tables—what kid would want to be around that?

A few young adults stated that they had encountered staff members who "really care." One young man who had lived at four different group homes stated that, at one home, "there was one staff member who was like a father to me. He really treated me as a son. He was a good guy. You don't have too many staff like that."

Two young adults who lived with foster families when arrested were placed into group homes by the court. One commented:

Judges don't understand that unless you're a strong-minded person, putting someone in a group home doesn't help them because that makes them feel even more like no one cares about them. Because those staff in group homes don't show you love either, so that just makes you like, "I don't care." Because there are people there who really don't care.

A second young adult whom the court placed into a group home stated, "Judges think the system is good for everyone, but they're just making monsters."

Young adults gave several examples of how the group home structure and the juvenile justice system fail to operate cohesively and, in some cases, further exacerbate the youth's problems. One young man stated that when he was given community service as a disposition:

The group home wouldn't help me get there. I would have to go AWOL to get to my community service. And my parole officer wasn't receptive to the fact that I was reliant on my group home to get me to community service.

Other young adults noted that they are put on AWOL status when they are arrested while living at a group home, and "when the kid gets out of jail, there's a warrant out for AWOL. They're on probation so they violate by being AWOL." Other young adults noted that "you can lose your bed in the group home because they think you're AWOL and you're in jail."

Experiences with Foster Families

Most of the young adults who lived with foster families when arrested were arrested for incidents that occurred outside the home, such as fighting at school. One youth was reported to the police by his foster mother, who claimed he attempted to sexually assault her birthchild (he claims they were engaged in consensual sexual activity).

Many young adults who lived with foster families felt that the families did not truly care for them. Young adults stated that their foster parents abused, belittled, and ignored them. One young man stated:

My foster parents said a lot of things that got me down—that's why I went to hustling. There were a lot of things that people didn't understand about me. My foster parents didn't know nothing—didn't know I was hustling, didn't know I had a gun in the house.

Another young adult said:

I always wanted to feel like I was their real family, and do things that the other kids got to do, like sit on the couch or get something to eat out of the refrigerator. I knew it wasn't my real family, but I wanted to feel like part of the family. Instead, I felt like I wasn't nothin.

Similarly, a young woman stated:

You're not receiving affection from the foster parents, not receiving the love you're looking for that you're missing on the inside. So you go outside looking for love on the street in the wrong places and that's how you get into trouble.

Another young adult said:

I got into trouble because of all the anger I have inside me— being in foster care is hard. My foster mother told everyone I was her foster kid and they all teased me. And not being with my family—I didn't know what was going on. I missed them and I didn't like anybody. I took being in foster care out on everybody.

Two young adults who lived with foster families at the time of their arrests were placed in group homes at disposition. One young woman felt strongly that her foster family "gave up on me and just didn't want to deal with me anymore." She was placed into a group home for a year, but when the year ended, "my foster parents decided they didn't want me back...so I had to stay there two years."

Who Attended Court Appearances with Youth, and Youths' Perceptions of How an Adult's Presence Affected Proceedings

Most young adults stated that no adult accompanied them when they appeared in court. One young man who was arrested while living in a group home stated that no one from the group home came to court with him. He said, "I had to go to court like five to six times and no one [from the group home] came with me. It was very painful to go through by myself." He stated that when he was arrested while living with a foster mother, "my foster mother came and advocated on my behalf."

One young man who was arrested multiple times while living in group care stated that no one from the group home accompanied him to any of his court proceedings. This young man said, "I had nobody in court on my behalf besides legal aid...The judge probably thought, if he gets out, he's probably gonna just cause more problems anyway." Another young man who was arrested multiple times while in group care stated that his caseworker from the group home came to court one time and that another time, someone from the group home picked him up from court. He described this individual as "a driver, not a caseworker...I don't know what he was there for." Another young man stated that the driver "just sits there and waits for you—to see if your case is dismissed or whatever." Other young adults agreed that a representative from the group home sometimes came to court to pick up youth and handle paperwork.

Some young adults who were living with foster families when arrested stated that their foster parents did not come to court with them. One young woman who was arrested twice while living with the same foster family stated that her foster mother did not come to court on the first charge. Her foster mother came to court on the second charge, but the case was remanded several times and, "she didn't want to put up with coming back to court so she didn't show up." That young woman commented:

They keep you there all day and she didn't want to sit there all day. I wouldn't want to sit there all day, but if it's somebody I care about, I'm gonna sit there. But she didn't care about me.

A young man who had been arrested numerous times stated that his foster mother came with him to court several times on one charge, but that she "only did it so it'd look good for her...All the other times, she was never there."

One young woman who was arrested while living with a foster family stated that her foster parents met with the judge and lawyers, and together, they decided on a disposition for her: to move into a group home. Despite the fact that her foster parents took an active role with the court, she felt "neglected...my foster parents never asked me what was right for me so that's just telling me that you don't care how I feel. They weren't concerned about my feelings...they didn't come talk to me about it."

Young adults generally believed that their foster parents did not appear with them in court because they "didn't care" about the youth or because they did not want to get involved with the courts. One young man stated:

When they called my foster mother, she wouldn't even come pick me up. She told me if I ever got caught doing bad stuff I was on my own...she knew what was going on but she said she wasn't getting into it.

Many young adults felt strongly that their foster parents did not care about them and were foster parents only for the income they received as foster parents. One young man stated, "Some people act like they want kids but they just want the money." A young woman stated that her foster parents "didn't want to go to court because they were private people...my foster mother really didn't care...it was all about the money."

Young adults felt strongly that the presence or absence of an adult advocating for them in court did have—or could have had—a significant effect on their court proceedings. Young adults who appeared in court without a foster parent, group home worker, or social worker felt that the court "wouldn't have been that hard on [me]" had an adult appeared and advocated for them. One young man stated, "I think they would have gone a little easier on me. But they see that I don't have nobody backing me up—they think, he's just a bad kid, throw him in the gutter and forget about him." Another young man stated, "The judge thinks, 'He's got no family, he's just running the streets, lock him up'...If your parents were there then they know there's someone to look after you." Another young adult stated:

I wanted to see somebody that I knew. And if they come, it shows the judge that you have somebody—that they are still working with you. But if nobody shows up, it looks like nobody cares about you and the judge thinks you are so bad that nobody wants to deal with you.

The same young adult noted, "Most of the kids who go to court are dependent on the social worker being there. There have been times when the judge would have let me out but the social worker didn't show up." Another young adult said:

I think judges don't let a lot of kids go—especially from group homes—especially if you go to court with [no one] on your side. All that says is that when you go back out there, you have no guardians and are gonna get in trouble again. They think I'm gonna go do something else because there was nobody in court with me.

Similarly, a young woman reported:

[My foster mother wasn't there] so they were like, well, nobody's here for her, send her away. If she had been there, they [might have] given me probation, but instead there's no adult there to say they'll watch me and make sure I go to probation.

Two young adults spoke of the anticipation of waiting to see if someone was coming to court with them. One young adult, who lived with a foster mother, stated, "I thought, she's gonna come—it was like having Santa Claus come—she's gonna come and watch, she's gonna get me out. And she never came." Another young adult, who lived in a group home, stated:

Most staff members say, "I can't make that court date, but I'll be there next time," and then they don't come next time. In reality, they don't want to come. Stop getting my hopes up and say you're going to come...I'm behind bars already...my court date could be tomorrow and I'm thinking, "Is she gonna come?" Instead of saying you're gonna come and then not come, just say you're not gonna come.

Two young adults stated that an adult appearing in court with them did make a difference in their dispositions. One young man stated, "I probably would have done the whole bit if it hadn't been for the social worker stepping in and saying I was a good kid." Another young man said that when his foster mother came with him to court, "it did help me out."

Young Adults' Experiences in Jail

Most young adults who spent time in jail described the experience in negative terms: "It was hell," "the worst week of my life," and "It was horrible—I would have rather slept outside." One young woman stated that she "lost all respect" for herself when she was in jail because she was treated badly there.

One young man stated that he "wasn't afraid of jail, because life in the group home had equipped me for that." That young man, who described himself as an advocate for alternatives to incarceration for adolescents, stated, "If you put a kid in detention who is still forming, they are just going to come out better at what they were doing...you just become a worse criminal." One young woman stated that being in jail

had a positive effect—I was scared and I was like, I'm never going back. It was like reality set in. People in there were telling me what not to do. It made me think not just about my situation then but about life itself.

Legal Representation

Most young adults had a court-appointed lawyer present at their court proceedings. The majority of young adults agreed that the lawyers "just want you to plead guilty," "don't care if you're innocent," and "don't really care." One young man, however, stated that he was satisfied with his lawyer.

Young People's Recommendations

Young adults made the following recommendations. Some recommendations focused on foster family placements and others on group home placements, although some of the recommendations were more general.

Recommendations for Foster Parents

• Require foster parents to attend classes on effective interaction with adolescents.

- Require foster parents to attend court with the children in their care.

- Encourage foster parents to engage in activities with the youth in their care so the youth are out on the street less often.

- Screen prospective foster parents more carefully.

Recommendations for Group Home Staff

- Educate group home staff about the legal system.

- Require that group home staff automatically check on a child who is detained by the juvenile justice system.

- Require group home staff who are knowledgeable about the youth to appear with the youth in court.

- Solicit input from youth about which group home staff members they want to appear with them in court.

- Provide group home staff with training so they do not call the police as a first resort for problems that occur in the group home.

- Ensure that group home staff expose youth in care to various experiences, such as reading books and discussing career options.

- Encourage group home staff to talk to youth about their futures.

- Mandate that social workers from the group home appear with the youth in court in addition to group home staff.

- Institute more thorough screening procedures when hiring group home staff.

- Improve group home conditions, and spend additional funds to hire more educated employees.

Recommendations to Benefit All Youth in Care

- Make mental health counseling available for youth in foster care.

- Require the court or police to automatically contact and advise the group home or foster parent when a youth who is in foster care is detained.

- Provide youth in foster care appearing on a delinquency petition with specialized legal services by an individual who is familiar with the foster care system and the juvenile justice system.

Focus Group and Follow-Up Interviews with Foster Parents

Seventeen foster parents participated in a focus group meeting. The foster parents were quite experienced: 1 foster parent had less than 5 years of experience; 3 had between 5 and 10 years of experience; and the remaining 13 had more than 10 years of experience. One married couple had 39 years of fostering experience. The researchers conducted phone interviews with two foster parents as a follow-up to the focus group. The comments of foster parents focused on the following areas:

- notification of the child's involvement with the juvenile justice system;

- calling the police;

- understanding the juvenile justice process;

- foster parents' roles in these situations;

- court participation; and

- other issues, including the quality of information on youths' backgrounds, legal liability, attitudes of social workers, legal representation of youth, and differential treatment of youth in foster care.

In addition, the foster parents offered advice for other foster parents caring for a youth who is charged with a delinquent act.

Notification of the Child's Involvement with the Juvenile Justice System

The foster parents recounted a range of circumstances in which children in their care became involved with the juvenile justice system. In one case, the child had stolen compact discs from a department store, and the police called the foster parent. In this foster parent's California community, the Foster Parent Association provides representatives who work directly with the police when these types of situations occur. The foster parent herself attended the court hearing, and the child received a fine, probation, and community service hours.

In another case, the child was arrested at school for "prank" activities. The school called the foster parent, and she in turn called the child's social worker. In this case, the foster parent commented that she wanted the child to understand that she did not condone the behavior, but she felt the disposition (weekend work for 24 weeks and two years of probation) was too harsh for a first offense.

Another foster parent reported that the sheriff's department appeared at her door and told her that her foster child had been arrested for stealing items valuing more than $1,000 from his school. The deputy sheriff asked if he could search the child's room. The foster parent contacted the social worker regarding whether to give permission, and the social worker authorized the foster parent to give the deputy sheriff access to the child's room, but the sheriff found nothing.

In another case, a 13-year-old girl on psychotropic medication and described by her foster parent as high risk left her foster home in California for Las Vegas. The foster parent alerted the agency to the child's runaway status, and the child's photo was posted on the Internet as a missing child. Police later arrested her in Las Vegas for prostitution and found her to be on drugs. The child's probation officer called the foster parent, who identified her as the child missing from her home. After the foster parent informed the probation officer that the child was on psychotropic medication, a nurse called for more information. The child was returned to California about three weeks later, with no hearing on the matter. The foster parent informed the agency that she was not willing for the child to return to her home. To her dismay, the social worker collected the child's things while the child waited in the car.

Another child was cited at school for committing an "assault with a deadly weapon," which turned out to be the child's tennis shoe. The child had kicked someone while having a disagreement. The foster parent was quite distressed that what she considered a relatively minor incident was treated as such a serious matter. She attended the child's hearing, believing it was important for her to be there because she knew the child well and could speak on his behalf.

In yet another school situation, a child assaulted the school principal, and the school called both the police and the foster parent. The foster parent felt that she needed to be an advocate for the child. She reported that the caseworker was helpful but did not understand how to handle the situation. The agency, however, did notify the foster parent about the hearing. The child ultimately was sent to a juvenile detention center.

In another case, two youth ages 13 and 16 were caught shoplifting at a department store. They were detained at the police station in an area with adults, and the police did not permit the foster parent to speak with them. The foster parent was outraged by this situation. (Another foster parent noted that in California, the law requires that a foster parent be allowed to speak with a detained child.) Later, the department store sent a letter to the foster parent, assessing the value of the goods. She informed the store that she was a foster parent, and at that point, the store dropped the entire matter. The foster parent stated that the store should have proceeded against the teens so that they would understand the consequences of their behavior.

A foster parent from California stated that when a youth in her care was arrested, she received written notice of the youth's delinquency court proceedings, sent with a return receipt requested.

Calling the Police and Understanding the Juvenile Justice Process

When asked how many foster parents had ever called the police to report a problem with children in their care, 13 of the 17 participants responded affirmatively. One foster parent, for example, reported to the police that two teens in her care were smoking marijuana in her home.

Not a single foster parent reported being given clear information regarding what to do if a child in a foster parent's care got into legal trouble. Most reported relying on informal support systems, other foster parents, or foster parent associations to understand what to do and how to respond to the police, the courts, and probation officers. They generally agreed that foster parents cannot rely on social workers for help in understanding what to do when a youth in their care is arrested.

A number of foster parents stated that they understood that if the child was in legal trouble, they were to call the child's social worker. One foster parent stated that in Illinois, the agency maintains a 24-hour-a-day, 7-day-a-week call-in system to handle calls from foster parents, including calls regarding a child's legal problems.

Foster parents from a Colorado county described an organization called The Hub, an interagency effort involving law enforcement and social services, that helps foster parents and others understand legal issues and what they can do on behalf of youth brought before the juvenile court. The foster parent who described this program stated that it works very well.

Foster Parents' Roles in These Situations

As a group, the foster parents endorsed the view that if a child in their care engaged in delinquent behavior or threatened the foster parent or anyone else, the foster parent should react as he or she would with a birthchild. As a group, the foster parents were adamant that they wished to participate in legal proceedings when a child in their care was charged with a delinquency offense. One foster parent asked, "If we don't, who will?" Another foster parent stated that it is the foster parent who is with the child around the clock, and asked, "Who can better represent them? The foster parent knows what youth need." Some foster parents were less certain about the advocacy role. One foster parent, for example, stated that she felt she "needed to advocate for [the youth] at times," but mostly felt her responsibility was to "just monitor him." Another foster parent described her role as "transporter and behavior historian."

One foster parent stated that many youth in foster care for whom she had cared were never hugged until they entered her home. She noted that many of the youth are high risk, angry, and out of control, and she stated that foster parents need to expect this type of behavior. Another foster parent remarked, "Kids need a family." Yet another foster parent commented that as a bus driver, he does not believe that these children are any different than the children he sees every day on his school bus. He stated, however, that children in foster care are more closely scrutinized than other children.

Court Participation

Almost all foster parents in the group stated that they had the opportunity to meet with probation officers, judges, prosecutors, and other court officials when children in their care were charged with delinquency offenses. About half of the group said that they had gone to court and spoken directly with the judge. Several foster parents described positive experiences in this regard. Foster parents from three different counties stated that they had been "well received" by the court system and that court officials asked them for their opinions. Another foster parent from a different community stated that the judge made a point of hearing from foster parents, and yet another foster parent described a situation in which a judge asked the foster parent to monitor how the youth progressed and advise the court.

Similarly, one foster parent reported a situation in which the judge asked the foster parent what the disposition should be. The foster parent believed that the youth needed jail time, and the judge followed the foster parent's suggestion. In another situation, the foster parent attended the initial hearing and told the court she did not believe that the child should be sent back home to her but should be in a juvenile corrections placement for the weekend. The court agreed and continued to elicit her advice throughout the process. Finally, one foster parent reported that she had written a letter to the court before the hearing for a child in her care. The judge read the letter and referenced it at the hearing. This foster parent stated that she has been "very lucky" with the court system, as the court listens to her.

Not all foster parents reported positive experiences with court personnel. One foster parent stated that she had met on a number of occasions with the child's probation officer. She felt that although she was treated with respect "at some level," particularly with regard to the information that she could share about the current status of the child, she was not taken seriously concerning the action that should be taken with regard to the child's offense. Her advice was not solicited on the steps that the court should take. She felt that there was not an overt disregard but rather a "that's nice" attitude toward her. Similarly, another foster parent stated, "I felt like the probation officer looked to the caseworker for more official information."

Foster parents agreed it is important that they get to know the judges and other court personnel and show that they support the courts. Foster parents remarked, "Foster parents' input can go a long way."

Despite the many positive stories that foster parents shared, as a group, they agreed that it is a 50-50 situation between being welcomed by the delinquency court and not being taken seriously.

Other Issues

In addition to the themes that emerged from the focus group and interviews, foster parents raised several other issues:

- **Limited information on youths' backgrounds.** Foster parents expressed distrust about how social workers portray youth with dangerous previous behaviors when attempting to place them with foster parents. One foster parent shared that a social worker had described a child as a "nice kid" when in reality, the child had been in more than 20 foster homes and had attempted to kill someone in a previous foster home. Another foster parent stated—and her statement was received with much agreement—that social workers do not fully share information on children until it is time to adopt. They had many complaints about the absence of full disclosure.

- **Legal liability.** One foster parent expressed a great deal of concern about the issues that she had to handle when a child in her care stole her car and caused an accident that resulted in personal injury and property damage. She highlighted the need to clarify the financial responsibility on the part of foster parents when these types of incidents occur.

  A number of foster parents expressed fear of civil judgments being rendered against them. One foster parent noted that foster parents are expected to use their homeowner insurance policies to cover damages caused by children in their care, but if they do, their rates increase.

- **Social workers' attitudes.** One foster parent stated that the courts are more responsive to youths' issues than are social workers. She described a situation in which a youth in her care stole compact discs from a social worker. The social worker came to the home and "threatened" the youth in ways that the foster parent found unacceptable. At least one foster parent stated that she had to end a placement because she could not get needed help or support from the social worker.

- **Legal representation of youth.** One foster parent emphasized the need for better legal representation of youth in foster care who are in delinquency court. She stated that these youth usually are represented by public defenders who do not give enough attention to their cases. This foster parent remarked that foster parents often cannot afford private lawyers, which leaves youth reliant on the public defender system. The foster parent also felt that the court treats youth who are represented by public defenders differently than youth who are represented by private attorneys.

- **Differential treatment of youth.** Two foster parents expressed the view that the delinquency court treats youth in foster care more harshly than youth who are not in foster care. One foster parent noted a racial bias on the part of police officers, and because many youth in foster care are from communities of color, the issue of race "compounds the problem."

- **Involvement of other foster parents.** One foster parent noted that there is a problem with foster parents who "are not involved" with the children in their care. She noted that these foster parents do little to keep youth out of trouble or advocate on their behalf if they do become involved with the delinquency court.

Foster Parents' Advice for Other Foster Parents

Foster parents offered the following advice for other foster parents who are caring for a youth who is charged with a delinquent act:

- Ask questions.

- Understand the policies and procedures of your state.

- Go to support groups.

- Don't hold anything back.

- Talk with the child's attorney.

- Advocate for the child, making certain that you are given the opportunity to provide feedback about the child's character and current behaviors.

- Pray a lot.

- In education and training programs, ask what to do if a child in your care gets into legal trouble.

- Address this issue at foster parent conferences.

Interviews
with Judges

Ten juvenile court judges participated in interviews. The interviews revealed significant variation in the operation of the juvenile courts over which the judges presided, with three models emerging. In some instances, courts reflect the "one family—one judge" model, wherein a youth's child welfare and delinquency proceedings are assigned to the same judge. In other instances, delinquency proceedings and child welfare proceedings proceed along parallel tracks in different courtrooms. And in other cases, when a youth may fall within the definitions of both *delinquent* and *dependent*, the jurisdiction uses a process to decide which court setting is more appropriate for that child. Under that approach, once police charge a child with an open child welfare case with a delinquent act, the probation department and social services meet and make a recommendation to the delinquency court as to which status the child should have. The judge makes the final decision, and the case proceeds accordingly. In this model, if the judge determines that the child's case should be before the delinquency court, the dependency court continues to hold jurisdiction until the youth is adjudicated delinquent.

The judges, who served in all three types of systems, focused on the following topics:

- judges' knowledge of youth's foster care status;

- the effect of foster care status on court proceedings;

- notice of proceedings;

- who, if anyone, attends court proceedings with youth, and how the presence or absence of an adult affects court proceedings; and

- disposition options for youth currently in foster care.

The judges also identified areas needing attention and made recommendations to improve the court's response to this population of youth.

Judge's Knowledge of Youths' Foster Care Status

Judges were divided on the extent to which they were aware of the fact that a youth appearing on a delinquency charge was currently in the foster care system. Some judges stated that they would know of the child's dependency background because automated computer information systems provide that information. In one judge's court system, each delinquent or dependent child's case is logged into an index, which courts can access to immediately identify that history. Other judges stated that they are aware of the child's foster care status in some cases but unaware in other cases. These judges stated that the information was available in a random manner. A judge commented:

> When the child gets arrested, the child doesn't necessarily say "I'm in foster care." At that point, there's no way for anybody to know. A lot of time it's by happenstance—there's not a procedure where the police would notify [foster parents]. [The youth] might give their foster parent's name but not identify them as a foster parent. So when they come to court, no one knows there's a foster parent because they haven't said that. Only by talking and doing more investigation, getting more answers, do we find out there's a foster home.

Another judge stated:

> The judge would have an idea a kid was in foster care if a kid had been detained prior to appearing. Because if a kid had been detained, it was likely due to the absence of the parent. Or if the kid showed up in court alone, in which case the judge would ask.

Another judge commented that the child may tell the police officer where he or she had been living, and the police may communicate that information to the court. One judge commented that she would know of the child's foster care background if a social worker appeared in court with the child or her probation staff informed her.

One judge whose system used the one family–one judge model stated that he likely would know the child's foster care status. He also said, however, that when a delinquency case is filed in a jurisdiction different from the jurisdiction where the child welfare case was filed, it was less likely that the judge would know of the child's foster care status.

Several judges whose courtrooms do not follow the one family–one judge model noted that even when they are aware of a youth's foster care status, they may be unaware of the status of the youth's siblings, which may be a placement consideration.

The Effect of Foster Care Status on Court Proceedings

Some judges stated that a youth's foster care status has some effect on delinquency court proceedings. According to a number of judges, a child with a foster care background may appear less stable to the court, which may affect decisions regarding the detention of youth prior to fact finding. One judge explained:

You're trying to look for some sort of stability. And there's an unfair perception that if a kid isn't in the home, he has less stability and you're more prone to have problems—even if it's a relative foster care placement. And so if the kid was with mom and dad (even if mom and dad weren't the best place for this child to be), it [would] probably [be] looked upon better than if the kid was in foster care. And so it probably is true that a judge [may think], "This kid isn't at home, he's gonna be a problem."

Judges also noted the child's being in foster care has implications regarding the child's release, if release is appropriate. One judge noted, "Sometimes if the child is placed on probation and can go home, the foster parents say 'I don't want the child back.' Then we have to figure out a placement for the child." Judges commented that a youth who normally would not be detained pending further proceedings faces the risk of detention when the court has no adult to whom it can release the youth. One judge said that his probation department was able to remedy that situation:

*Now, if a placement refuses to take a foster child back, proba-
tion will contact the child welfare agency, and the agency assumes responsibility for the child, who then need not be detained. Additionally, probation contacts the child's dependency
attorney, which engages the attorney in that process.*

One judge stated that a youth's foster care status was more likely to
be used in mitigation and that judges may be somewhat more lenient
toward youth who are in care. Another judge, however, stated, "I do
think it goes both ways [judges going easier and also being harder on
kids] based on the foster care background." The judge stated that people
have a perception that children in foster care grow up to be violent
criminals. Similarly, another judge noted:

*In my experience, foster care is just one of those preparatory
steps before the kid commits a crime. The vast majority of kids
who are in foster care will do something—trespassing, shoplift,
assault, smoking marijuana, whatever. If you get in foster care,
the risk factors go up and you'll probably see the kid in the
delinquency system.*

Notice of Proceedings

The judges who were interviewed reported different experiences regarding the court providing notice of hearings to adults involved with
youth in foster care. Some judges stated that notice of delinquency proceedings goes to the child's guardian, which is often the child welfare
agency. Other judges reported that the agency and, on occasion,
birthparents or foster parents, learned about delinquency proceedings
in a happenstance manner. Judges reported that notice of hearings often is the result of informal communications among the child, foster
parents, and social worker. One judge described the notification process as follows:

*We were required in our clerk's office of the juvenile court to
serve [notice on] the mother, the father, and whoever was the
custodian. So if the custodian was [the department of social
services], we served [them]—and that was required by law. What
we had difficulty with was mother's location/father's location,
because quite often [youth] would leave and not tell social services where they went to. If [youth] were in a group home, we*

sent the papers to the group home...Legal mother and legal fa-
ther—unless they had their rights terminated—they were en-
titled to notice. A lot of times [the department of social ser-
vices] did not know where they were. If a child was delinquent
and was in foster care in my county, then generally either the
child would say who their foster parents were or they would
say they are in [the department's] custody. And if they didn't,
the next day we would know they were in [the department's]
custody and the intake officer would contact [the department],
who would in turn contact the foster parents.

Another judge remarked that it is difficult for delinquency courts
to facilitate the involvement of foster parents or birthparents because
the delinquency court, unlike the dependency court, has limited control over children's birthparents and foster parents.

Judges' Perceptions of How an Adult's Presence Affects Court Proceedings

Judges had different experiences with regard to adults attending delinquency proceedings for youth in foster care. One judge described the
situation as "a crapshoot" and stated that it is unclear who will show
up for a youth in foster care. This judge added that caseworkers typically do not appear. Another judge stated that birthparents and foster
parents "don't show up...so it doesn't look real good, because without
mom and dad there, in theory, the kid isn't all that stable."

Judges pointed out a number of reasons why birthparents and foster
parents may not appear in court, including the possibility that the social workers or probation officers do not inform the parents in the belief
that they would not appear even if they were informed. Judges also
mentioned that foster parents may be angry with the child, may find the
court date inconvenient, or may be intimidated by what is "not a foster
parent– or any parent-friendly place." Another judge noted, however,
that although she has the power to subpoena foster parents, she found
that foster parents usually came to court on their own initiative.

Some judges stated that attorneys who represent youth in dependency proceedings also appear in delinquency court to advocate on
behalf of the youth. One judge, who described her jurisdiction as unusual, noted:

In 70% [of cases] or more, the dependency lawyer shows up with the kid. I couldn't tell you what number of people have somebody from their foster home or somebody from case management but a significant proportion of them—maybe 60%–70% do. It would be very unusual for a child to not have the social worker there—we continue [the case] so the social workers can be present...And sometimes we will "notice" the parents and the parents will come—it's pretty unusual to have no adults there. If you count the dependency lawyer, I'd say about 80% [of kids currently in foster care have an adult besides a lawyer appear in court with them].

Another judge stated that an adult "always" appears with the child in court and attributed the frequent adult presence to the fact that the court sent summonses to the child's legal mother, legal father, and custodian. The judge recalled a case in which the foster parent appeared, but the caseworker did not:

I had my clerk call and ask, "Where is your worker? Why isn't somebody from [the child welfare agency] here, you are the legal custodians and the judge wants you here." They said, "We're not coming." The clerk said, "If you don't come, the judge is going to issue a show-cause for contempt against you; you are legally obligated to be here, you are the custodian of this child."

Another judge said that she can continue the proceedings if the legal guardian is not present, and occasionally she does that when a youth is facing a serious charge. Other judges stated that the presence of adults varies depending on the proceeding, noting that foster parents and caseworkers are most useful to the court at the dispositional phase of proceedings, when information they can provide may help the court make an informed decision about the child. Judges reported that when caseworkers do appear with children, they sometimes are active participants in the judicial process and sometimes are present only to transport the youth.

Some judges minimized the effect of the absence of any adults on behalf of the child. These judges emphasized the value of the probation report or assessment—developed by probation officials or both probation officials and child welfare workers—which contains an assessment of the child and a disposition recommendation. Judges remarked that the reports are most useful when workers prepare them jointly, as opposed to the probation officer and the child welfare worker preparing separate reports that they then merge into one document. One judge remarked, "It really doesn't matter that much whether or not someone is there or not because the court has received this joint assessment which is required to have all this information in it." Not all judges agreed on the value of these assessments, however, finding them sometimes very cursory or incomplete.

Disposition Options for Youth Currently in Foster Care

Judges agreed that the principle of "the least restrictive placement setting that is in the best interest of the child" guided their dispositional decisionmaking. They also agreed that when a judge assesses options for a child in foster care, he or she must consider the appropriateness of returning the child to that setting. In this regard, judges stated:

> If the kid commits a crime while in foster care, then there's a problem with foster care. So then you look at group home and/or out-of-home placement or some sort of detention. So you might rule out the home right off the bat because the kid did something while in foster care. Most times you will think...the home isn't good, and so if the kid isn't making it in foster care we should look at group home or jail.

> If the kid is in foster care and then gets arrested, it doesn't look like control is being provided at the placement—especially if the crime is late at night—it looks like the placement is unsuitable. So a more structured foster care placement might be needed.

Another judge described the disposition options as such:

> If the foster family would take them back, we would put additional specialized services in the home. We would perhaps do an inpatient mental health evaluation, which might give us a new perspective on how to work with that child. The next step would be therapeutic foster care. Next would be our local group home, which would leave the child in the community but give them more structure and discipline. Next would be residential placement for special-needs children. Next we would keep them

at our detention center under certain limited circumstances for up to six months and infuse treatment into the detention center. Last alternative would be commitment to the department of juvenile justice, which is something you don't want to do when you know the child is in the foster care system [because you know that they wouldn't be in the foster care system had they not been abused or neglected]...Sometimes if they are in a group home, the group home will take them back with intensive services.

One judge noted that youth who are in foster care often have "baggage," such as problems at school or a history of running away, that is relevant to detention, disposition, and probation decisions. The judge said that when considering disposition options, family involvement is an important factor: A youth whose family is involved is more likely to receive an alternative to detention than a youth with similar problems who does not have family involvement. This judge noted that many of the programs that are alternatives to detention focus on family involvement, and youth whose families are not engaged would not be considered for these programs.

Finally, one judge stated that in his observation, the percentage of youth with a foster care background who receive informal supervision as a disposition is consistent with the percentage of youth overall who receive that disposition. This judge pointed to data that indicates that youth with a foster care background are not perceived differently at disposition.

Recommendations

Judges made recommendations in several areas:

- the role of the guardian ad litem (GAL) or court-appointed special advocate (CASA) volunteer,

- court procedure,

- child welfare system and juvenile justice system coordination,

- adult involvement in youth's lives, and

- other issues.

- **The role of the GAL or CASA volunteer.** Judges frequently mentioned the benefit of having a GAL or CASA accompany the child into delinquency proceedings. Judges recognized that according to the national mandate, GALs and CASAs are intended only for dependency proceedings, however, judges repeatedly commented that these advocates are excellent resources in delinquency proceedings. Among their comments were:

  We find that outcomes for children are better when there's somebody advocating for [youth] in the court system who is personally familiar with them—it's like they are the conscience of the system. CASAs can give so much more information than the social workers, even when the social workers are really good, because they spend so much more time.

  The national mandate says that CASAs are only in dependency cases—not delinquency cases—so the question arises, if a CASA has a child in a dependency case, and that child then gets a delinquency case, does that mean the CASA can't go sit with the child in the delinquency case? Because that's what the child needs. We do not have the ability to assign a CASA to a delinquency case. And that is one way to get some continuity in the case.

  Even if you have a defense attorney, they most likely would just be arguing the defense part of the case—they wouldn't argue placement, foster care—so without the GAL, you have that part of the equation missing—that is, where is this kid best placed?

- **Court procedure.** Judges agreed that a system is needed to allow judges to immediately learn whether a child appearing before them is in foster care. Similarly, they emphasized that caseworkers should receive immediate notification of detention and notice of court dates, and caseworkers should be required parties in delinquency cases. One judge remarked, "The caseworker is the stand-in for the parents, and the caseworker should be everywhere that a parent would be required to be. They should attend all the hearings and really know what's going on with the child."

Judges often mentioned the appeal of the one family–one judge model. One judge stated:

> *You should have one court–one family; you shouldn't have multiple judges deciding the case. So if you have a [dependency and neglect case], a delinquency case, a truancy case, whatever, you should have one court hearing the case because then that court and that judge will have enough history about the kid and the family that he can make a more-informed decision about the kid than a judge that's just hearing one side of the case and not the other.*

Two judges pointed out impediments to the model, however, noting that judges who currently preside over dependency court proceedings may not want to try criminal cases. Another judge noted that in her jurisdiction, the one family–one judge model was not embraced because "we are all so specialized." Nonetheless, judges agreed on the need for access to information on dependency court proceedings and on the need for dependency court judges to have access to delinquency court records.

Judges also mentioned that lawyers who represent children should be familiar with both child welfare and juvenile delinquency law. One judge expressed:

> *The lawyers who are representing these kids need to have a knowledge base in both fields. Even if they are excellent trial lawyers on the criminal side, they cannot really do justice by their clients unless they have some knowledge about the other side.*

Several judges mentioned the desirability of having one attorney represent the child in both dependency and delinquency cases. Judges emphasized that at a minimum, the child's dependency and delinquency court attorneys should be working together for the child.

Several judges mentioned the need for cross-training of judges. One judge stated:

> *There has to be tremendous training of judges; there has to be cross training. It can't be that the judges are trained separately from the probation officers or social workers—there should be a team approach to training, which is hard to do because of all the territorialness. But unless everyone is on the same page, it won't work. The focus ought to be earmarked toward a training*

program that would include a judge, a probation officer, social worker, GAL, the whole group at one time. Having [district attorneys] involved is important too.

- **Child welfare system and juvenile justice system coordination.** Judges emphasized that although some progress has been made, courts must do more in terms of clarifying roles for caseworkers and probation officers. One judge commented:

  Sometimes there is a perception among caseworkers that if a delinquency case starts, they are not involved in that. And it goes the same way with probation—if it's a dependency case, the probation officer thinks, "Now that it's a dependency case, I am off of the hook." There should not be an assumption on the part of either the caseworker or the probation officer that they get a handoff because there is another case.

Judges acknowledged the relationship between funding of services and the determination of the system or court with jurisdiction over the child. One judge felt that her system was a good model—in her state, all children's cases (dependency and delinquency) are presented to a multidisciplinary team including both probation staff and child services staff. The team makes funding recommendations if in-home or out-of-home services are required but are not available through agency staff. The judge believes that this structure "makes all agencies own every child and avoids 'this is my pot of money, that is yours' thinking."

- **Adult involvement in youth's lives.** Judges also emphasized the vital role of caring adults in youth's lives:

  The more connected the kid is to a family person—whether it's "grandma foster care" or whatever—the more connection you have to an actual relative, the less likely that kid will reoffend. Now that's not always true because if the family is just as dysfunctional as mom and dad, then you have the same ongoing issues. But it's my belief that if a kid is in [kinship] foster care he will have a better chance of surviving than if he is in stranger foster care.

  They have to have at least one adult who considers it one of the primary responsibilities of their life to help this kid [make it].

They also stressed the importance of all the adults active in a child's life being present in court and the need for better methods of ensuring the presence of the foster family, birthparents, and the social worker.

- **Other issues.** Several judges mentioned the need for a vehicle to ensure a child's return to the dependency system once the delinquency case is resolved. One judge, however, stated that the delinquency court—not the dependency court—should have planning responsibility when the child exits the juvenile justice system:

  > *We should not be sending the kid back to the dependency system; the delinquency system should be making all the arrangements and preparing for permanency for this kid. But the delinquency system is not traditionally set up to do that.*

Judges also noted that a secure placement is often extended because a foster care placement for the youth has not been identified.

Judges commented that a delinquency petition is often the precipitating cause of a dependency petition. Youth who initially appear in court on delinquency charges may be placed in foster care because their families are unable or unwilling to care for them. One judge remarked:

> *I think that there's quite a bit of overlap between kids who are in foster care and delinquency, but it's hard to tell what comes first—we have some children who are in delinquency first and then they end up in foster care. Like when a child has three or four delinquency cases and the parent says, "I can't do it— I want to give the child up because of their delinquency background." It goes both ways.*

Interviews with
Public Child Welfare
Administrators

Five public child welfare administrators in five different states participated in phone interviews. Their comments focused on the following issues:

- the role of the child welfare system when a youth in care becomes involved with the juvenile justice system,

- factors that affect a child welfare caseworker's involvement in juvenile delinquency proceedings,

- dynamics that impede the ability of child welfare and juvenile justice systems to coordinate efforts when a youth in care is charged with a delinquent act,

- dynamics that facilitate the ability of child welfare and juvenile justice systems to coordinate efforts when a youth in care is charged with a delinquent act, and

- sources of tension between the child welfare and juvenile justice systems when a youth in care is arrested for a delinquent act.

The Child Welfare System's Role When a Youth Is Involved with Juvenile Justice

Administrators agreed that when a youth in care becomes involved with the juvenile justice system, the child welfare system should continue to play a role in the child's life until a judge decides otherwise. Administrators stated that the child welfare system's involvement should end only "when the judge transfers custody of the youth from child welfare to juvenile justice," "when the judge releases the child welfare system," or "when the judge makes a judicial finding that our services are no longer needed." One administrator stated, "When [the youth] are arrested and in detention, they are still ours...we close the case when a child goes into the custody of [the juvenile justice system]." These administrators stated they had a clear understanding of when responsibility for a child shifts from the child welfare system to the juvenile justice system. One administrator stated:

> If we are active with the juvenile court, and a kid comes in for a delinquency proceeding, we don't close our case—that's our policy—until the juvenile court judge says to close the case. It is a pretty clear process.

Administrators indicated that agencies have moved away from previous beliefs about the role of the child welfare system in these circumstances. In the past, the child welfare system took the position that it had no responsibility once a child became involved with the delinquency court, and child welfare caseworkers took a hands-off approach when a youth in care was arrested. An administrator said, "We used to think that if a child went into juvenile justice—especially if they went into some type of incarceration—they were gone forever, and the system just closed up." Another administrator described current thinking in this way: "We view it as our role to attempt to provide services to the child and the family so they can expedite their exit out of both child welfare and delinquency." One administrator, however, stated that changes in practice have been slow to occur: "When a kid goes into juvenile justice, [the caseworker] might keep the case open but for the most part, [the attitude is] 'no longer on my caseload, I am done with this one.'" Another administrator noted that the role of the child welfare system lessens when youth are arrested but stated some responsibilities remain:

> I would love to say that we wrap our children pretty tight and support them but in reality, when they become known to the juvenile justice system, different provisions of the state code take over and the other system has things it has to do.

This administrator stated that in her system, caseworkers attempt to continue working with families, ensure that youth understand their rights, take supplies to youth when they are detained, and work with youth to make sure they understand what is happening to them.

Most of the child welfare administrators cited an increased awareness of the child welfare system's responsibility for case planning when youth exit the juvenile justice system. One administrator stated:

> *If we are the initial custodial agency and then the child becomes involved in the juvenile justice system, when they serve their time...custody reverts back to us, so it's important for us to maintain some sort of awareness of those children because we're going to have to pick up case planning responsibility when they come back.*

Two administrators stated that their departments view delinquency as "another service need" to which the child welfare system can respond. One administrator noted:

> *We don't see delinquency [in] a vacuum...there may be other conditions that the child welfare system should address, such as school, interaction with the family, tangible services or counseling...we see our role as a collaborative one that is in the best interests of the child, and we don't see delinquency as separate from other issues or pressing needs that have to be addressed with the [youth].*

Similarly, one juvenile justice administrator who participated in an interview with a child welfare administrator noted, "Over the last year, I saw more of the [child welfare] workers tracking us down, saying, 'I am the person responsible for this child and I want to know what your plans are and what's going on.'"

Factors that Affect a Worker's Involvement in Delinquency Proceedings

Child welfare administrators stated that the role a caseworker plays once a youth in care has been arrested varies as a result of several factors, including the caseworker's motivation level. They stated that caseworkers are most motivated to advocate on behalf of youth when they have been working with the youth for a long period of time. An administrator noted:

If it's a new case or a new caseworker, I see workers not really going out there in terms of trying to advocate for the child or remain involved. Yet, I've seen cases where the same worker has had the child on their caseload for five to six years and you'll see a worker who is a lot more actively involved in that case...If the caseworker has had this case for six months or longer, I think you will see more activity in terms of the worker being engaged, because they will have had an opportunity to develop a relationship with that child.

Administrators also noted that caseworkers may be more reluctant to advocate on behalf of a youth if the charges against the youth are very serious, the worker's caseload is large and time consuming, or they feel their safety is at issue. Administrators agreed that caseworkers are more likely to be active in the youth's case and appear in delinquency court if they feel well received by the juvenile court. Several administrators noted that caseworkers are more likely to appear when the juvenile court judge specifies that their presence is desired. Administrators also pointed to the relationship between the probation worker and the caseworker:

Sometimes the [probation officer] seeks out the caseworker for information. It depends on the [probation officer] and their attitude about us...Other times, we have to reach out to them and sometimes they are receptive to our input, sometimes they are not.

It does kind of depend upon the credibility and experience of the foster care worker. Also on the experiences that the probation officer or prosecutor has had in the past with our agency. It seems to me that relationships are what's critical—if you've been around for awhile and you have developed relationships with these people, then they are more likely to want to involve you and to listen to you.

Administrators also pointed to a lack of notice of proceedings as one reason that caseworkers may not attend delinquency proceedings for a youth currently in foster care. Administrators reported wide variation in the extent to which they receive notice of delinquency proceedings. In some instances, administrators reported that the clerk of the courts automatically notifies them. By contrast, one administrator reported that the agency once learned of a youth's delinquency proceeding by reading about the outcome of the proceeding in the newspaper.

Other administrators reported that in some cases, the caseworker relies on the foster parent, residential home worker, or probation worker for notification of delinquency court proceedings.

Dynamics that Impede System Coordination When a Youth Is Charged with a Delinquent Act

Administrators identified several factors as impediments to the cohesive functioning of the juvenile justice and child welfare systems when a youth in care is charged with a delinquent act. Most frequently, administrators cited the different missions of the two systems. One juvenile justice administrator who participated in an interview with a child welfare administrator noted, "We do welcome child welfare participation, but there are some different agendas in terms of what needs to be accomplished when a child is delinquent compared to being only a dependent child." Administrators also frequently mentioned caseworkers' and probation officers' lack of understanding about the role of the other system and individual worker. One administrator noted:

> Part of what we can do better is having our staff understand each other's system. Sometimes when there are problems, it is not a matter of not wanting to work together, it's a matter of child welfare not understanding the role of the probation officer, and vice versa. We have begun some cross-trainings in order to better understand each other's systems and we need to continue to do that. That is a barrier—while the mission is to protect the interests of the child and the community, sometimes we don't understand how we arrive at that—and cross-systems training helps that.

A child welfare administrator noted that sometimes caseworkers lack an understanding of the juvenile justice system:

> Workers need to understand what a secure setting means in a child's life. If they knew what it meant, they might advocate a little stronger for the child. So the worker needs a better understanding of what the legal consequences are for different actions.

Administrators repeatedly mentioned the following factors as impeding the coordination between child welfare and juvenile justice systems:

- philosophical differences between the juvenile justice and child welfare systems, with juvenile justice having a more punitive approach;

- siloed processes of the two systems;

- caseworkers' unfamiliarity with and fear of the delinquency court process;

- caseworkers' fear of youth who commit delinquent acts;

- caseworkers' and probation officers' lack of understanding about the role of the other system;

- role confusion on the part of individual caseworkers;

- the focus of the system, with child welfare focusing on the whole family and juvenile justice focusing on the individual youth;

- judges who lack child welfare training; and

- judges who sit on the juvenile court bench only because it is the starting point for judges and who lack an interest in these issues.

Dynamics that Facilitate the Coordination of Child Welfare and Juvenile Justice When a Youth Is Charged with a Delinquent Act

Administrators identified several factors that facilitate collaboration between the juvenile justice and child welfare systems. Most frequently, administrators noted the benefit of familiarity and communication between child welfare and juvenile justice staff. One administrator commented:

> We are trying to get our people to know one another—to get supervisors in probation to know their counterparts in [child] welfare and get them to have joint meetings and conversations—get them to know one another so when there's an issue they can just pick up the phone and talk it over so things don't blow up in court.

Administrators also frequently mentioned the following factors as facilitating the collaboration of child welfare and juvenile justice systems:

- agency directors who expect collaboration;

- clear statutes and written protocols that define the roles of the two systems in serving the youth;

- periodic joint meetings of child welfare and juvenile justice staff;

- joint training of child welfare and juvenile justice staff;

- courts' acknowledgment of the roles of both systems, and courts' respect for the child welfare system;

- an organizational mindset on the part of both the child welfare and juvenile justice agencies that values joint planning;

- cross-training of caseworkers and probation officers, which encourages understanding of the other system;

- the creation of multisystem teams that engage in joint planning for the youth;

- judges who have several years of judicial experience serving on the bench of juvenile courts;

- judges who call together child welfare and juvenile justice staff for meetings on individual cases;

- courts that follow the one family–one judge model;

- protocols that allow for automatic notice to the child welfare system when police arrest a child in foster care for a delinquent act;

- a statutory requirement that the delinquency court hear from the child welfare system regarding the services that have been provided to the youth; and

- information systems that allow child welfare caseworkers to access juvenile justice records and allow juvenile justice staff to access child welfare records.

Sources of Tension Between Child Welfare and Juvenile Justice When a Youth Is Charged with a Delinquent Act

Child welfare administrators identified several sources of tension between the child welfare and juvenile justice systems. They indicated that judges may keep youth in the child welfare system because therapeutic services are more readily available in that system. An administrator stated:

Because of funding and access to services, the courts will very often leave the case in the charge of the neglect worker. There will still be a probation officer there, but the foster care worker will carry out the service plan we've developed. Then the court won't have to pay for the services or staff the case as intensely as it might have had to otherwise. There is a tendency to leave kids with foster care so that our resources can be used to meet the needs of the kids, especially if the current placement can be maintained.

Yet administrators pointed to the difficulty of finding placements in the child welfare system that will accept children who have been in trouble with the law. One administrator noted, "There's a real fear that if a child develops any type of juvenile justice portfolio, that child is going to be really difficult to serve in the child welfare system, regardless of what the issues are."

Administrators also noted the tendency of some judges to order joint planning or dual supervision for a child, which requires child welfare and juvenile justice professionals to work together in making recommendations to the court. Administrators agreed that both approaches are good in theory, but they "only work if there is trust and respect." One juvenile justice administrator described the challenge that results when case planning responsibility becomes divided between the two systems:

The real challenge comes when the caseworker may continue to work with family (there could be other kids in the family in foster care or at home receiving preventive services)...so the caseworker's life becomes more complicated because they are the case planner for mom and dad and the kids but [juvenile justice has] responsibility to plan for the youth. The challenge is to create a seamless single case plan for the whole family.

Administrators pointed to the need for established protocols that specify the type of notice a child welfare agency is entitled to receive when a youth exits the juvenile justice system. One administrator noted:

When a child goes into the custody of [the department of juvenile justice], we close our foster care case, and then we pick them back up again when they come out—but we might not know they are coming out until that day of discharge.

A juvenile justice administrator acknowledged the problem:

At month 6 or 7 when we start our discharge planning with kids, all of a sudden we find out that we do not have a home for that child to go back to—we have had no communication with the county whatsoever—and that kid could end up spending a lot longer in residential care than they would normally need to do because the planning has not been done at all...In some cases, the county refuses to become involved in the discharge planning for the child because they say, "They are with you and until they're not with you, we're not getting involved." Yet we have no place for that child to go back to unless the county is involved with us. It's kind of like we chase each other around the block as far as who is responsible for it.

Juvenile Justice/ Child Welfare Coordination: Innovative Programs

Despite the frequently made recommendation that child welfare and juvenile justice systems coordinate their efforts, few programs are designed to accomplish this goal. The authors conducted research to identify programs that attempt to coordinate services for youth involved in both the child welfare and juvenile justice systems and to assess the implementation of these programs and the results they have achieved.

The link between the child welfare and juvenile justice agencies will become even more important as a result of federal mandates in the reauthorized Juvenile Justice and Delinquency Prevention Act (JJDPA), originally signed into law in 1974 and reauthorized in 2002. This law requires states to develop policies and systems to incorporate relevant child protective service records into juvenile justice records. The legislation also requires that the federal government undertake a study of how juvenile justice and child welfare systems are, in fact, coordinating services and treatment.

An NCJJ study included a survey of 94 jurisdictions across the United States to identify promising practices for youth who are involved in both the child welfare and juvenile justice systems. Results from this survey are expected to be available in the fall of 2004, but preliminary results indicate that although respondents believed it important for jurisdictions to have effective program responses in dual jurisdiction cases, few such programs exist (Gene Siegel, personal communication, January 22, 2004). Similarly, the Child Welfare League of America has identified a variety of efforts to coordinate the work of multiple systems, but it continues to emphasize the need for integration of youth-serving systems to ensure a more adequate response to youth who are involved in both the juvenile justice and child welfare systems (Wiig, Widom, & Tuell, 2003).

This report highlights several programs:

- New York City: Project Confirm

- Iowa: Decategorization Project and Comprehensive Strategy Process

- Milwaukee: Wraparound Milwaukee

- Cook County, Illinois: Judicial committee and database

- Kentucky: Interagency memorandum of understanding

- Hennepin County, Minnesota: Project and juvenile assessment center

- California: Joinder law and a coordinated system

- Kansas City, Missouri: KidSafe Program

- Michigan: The Juvenile Justice Online Technology system

The coordination efforts discussed here have used a number of strategies, such as blending funding streams, creating policy and funding incentives to improve outcomes, auditing systems to eliminate overlap in service delivery, providing crossover case management, developing shared information systems, and implementing the one family–one judge court model.

Following the descriptions of these programs, the authors describe recent changes in two federal laws that reflect a growing recognition of the connection between child maltreatment and delinquency and that provide opportunities for states to enhance their interagency collaboration.

New York City: Project Confirm

The most clearly defined effort to link child welfare and juvenile justice systems is the Vera Institute's Project Confirm based in New York City. The program began as a research collaboration with New York City's public child welfare agency, Administration for Children's Services (ACS), with the goal of diagramming the movement of juveniles among the child welfare, juvenile justice, mental health, and status-offender systems. The study documented the extent to which children are involved in multiple systems and the lack of mutual understanding and cooperation among the agencies that serve them. The Vera Institute (Conger & Ross, 2001) issued a series of reports that revealed that although youth in the custody of ACS committed comparatively less serious offenses than youth who were not in ACS custody, courts detained them at a higher rate. This finding led to the conclusion that biases worked against youth in care with regard to dispositional decisions. The researchers surmised that when teenagers outside the foster care system are arrested, their parents are usually on hand to take them home, but when children in foster care are arrested, typically, no one assumes responsibility for them.

These research findings led to the development of Project Confirm in 1998, a process by which child welfare and juvenile justice agencies communicate and work together toward reducing the detention bias against children in foster care. Two major components were implemented: notification and court consultation. The notification component ensures that as soon as a juvenile is arrested in New York City, the project's staff reviews child welfare records to determine if the youth is in foster care. If so, the staff notify a liaison at the appropriate private foster care agency (or the ACS case manager, if the youth is in a placement operated by ACS) and inform him or her of the obligation to appear with the youth in court.[3] The agency liaison then instructs the youth's caseworker to call Project Confirm for more information. The court consultation component provides project staff who guide agency staff through the court process. The results from Project Confirm have been encouraging. The rate of appearance by custodians and child welfare workers has increased, and the foster care bias has been eliminated in detention decisions for youth charged with low-level offenses and with no prior records. In 2001, ACS assumed responsibility for the operation of Project Confirm. Other states are studying the program, looking to implement similar systems in their jurisdictions.

Iowa: Decategorization Project and Comprehensive Strategy Process

Efforts to improve coordination between the child welfare and juvenile justice systems in Iowa began with the Decategorization Project, which had as its goal the consolidation of traditional funding streams for county child and family services into a single child welfare fund. The state recognized that its fragmented system of service programs offered services based on funding availability rather than families' actual needs, and it sought to make systemic reforms to better coordinate services. In 1997, six/Iowa communities participated in the Office of Juvenile Justice and Delinquency Prevention's (OJJDP) Comprehensive Strategy training and technical assistance initiative. Following that effort, the Iowa Division of Criminal and Juvenile Justice Planning met with state and local agency personnel to design comprehensive plans to link the child welfare and juvenile justice systems, allocate resources, and deliver services more effectively. The plan for each of the six sites prioritizes risk factor areas and identifies resources and gaps in services for youth involved in both the child welfare and juvenile justice systems. Sites are working on implementing their five-year plans, and OJJDP continues to support their efforts by providing assessments and site-specific training and technical assistance.

Milwaukee: Wraparound Milwaukee

Wraparound Milwaukee is a comprehensive system of care that includes the mental health, child welfare, juvenile justice, and educational services systems to address the complex needs of youth with severe emotional, behavioral, and mental health problems, many of whom have been adjudicated delinquent. Wraparound plans are family driven. The program provides a care coordinator who conducts assessments and helps identify needed services (with one coordinator for eight families), a mobile crisis team, and a service provider network that responds to multiple needs through 60 different services. Children who are involved in the juvenile justice, child welfare, and mental health systems are served through a public managed care organization that offers a comprehensive benefit plan. In 1999, the child welfare and juvenile justice systems funded Wraparound Milwaukee in the amount of $3,300 per month, per child. In addition, a $1,542 per month, per child capitation payment from Medicaid covered the projected cost for mental health and substance abuse services. Due to its blended funding approach, Wraparound Milwaukee provides a flexible, comprehensive menu of services to youth who are adjudicated delinquent. This program's outcomes have been positive: The use of residential treatment has lessened and the recidivism rate has decreased.

Cook County, Illinois: Judicial Committee and Database

In 2000, presiding judges of the juvenile courts in Cook County, which separately handle child welfare cases and delinquency cases, established a committee to examine the system response to dually involved minors. The committee aimed to encourage cooperation between probation officers and caseworkers and ensure better legal representation of minors. It created a database to track dually involved minors and to improve the flow of information between the court divisions. Slavin (2001) reported that delinquency court judges and probation officers use the database to communicate with child welfare workers and attorneys. Slavin further reported that child welfare caseworkers appear in delinquency court more often than they did previously and that courts have begun same-day scheduling of child welfare proceedings and delinquency hearings, which has the added benefit of encouraging teenagers to attend their permanency hearings.

Kentucky: Interagency Memorandum of Understanding

Kentucky began implementation of its collaborative programming between child welfare agencies and juvenile justice departments when the state's juvenile justice department was separated from the agency that once handled both child welfare and juvenile justice. As problems in communication and coordination became apparent, the child welfare and juvenile justice agencies formed a working group with representatives from both agencies and forged an agreement under which problems would be addressed. The group created a memorandum of understanding (MOU) in 1999 that documented an agreement that all decisions would be made in the best interests of the child and that both agencies would work to assist the efforts of the other agency. The MOU states that child welfare and juvenile justice staff will work to agree on a disposition for a dually involved child, with the final decision made by the judge. It provides that committing a child to the juvenile justice agency as a public offender will not terminate the jurisdiction of the child welfare agency. Furthermore, it allows for the sharing of records between agencies. Kentucky's MOU offers a good example of joint child welfare and juvenile justice efforts to establish clear rules and a defined process for working with youth who are involved in both systems.

Hennepin County, Minnesota: Project and Juvenile Assessment Center

In Hennepin County, Minnesota, the court identifies children who are involved in both the child welfare and juvenile justice systems. One attorney represents the child in both the dependency and delinquency aspects of the case, although the court also may appoint a GAL. The judge has the file of the family at his or her disposal when making decisions about the child. The child is served by a probation officer and a child welfare social worker who work together to decide which agency will take the lead and have access to the court's file on the entire family.

Prior to 2002, Hennepin County began planning for a juvenile assessment center (JAC) as a single point of entry through which workers could mobilize the services of multiple agencies. The plan included the provision of needs assessments for youth who are delinquent or at risk of becoming delinquent, considering the youth's needs in relation to all systems that potentially may be involved in a treatment plan (including juvenile justice, mental health, education, and child welfare). The plan also included a comprehensive, integrated management information system with a centralized database to provide assessment information on the youth and the services provided to the youth. The legislature, however, repealed the law granting funding for the Hennepin County JAC in 2002. The county's plan for the creation of the JAC may be of use to prospective JAC sites. Model JACs currently exist in two Florida counties, Miami-Dade County and Hillsborough County.

California: Joinder Law and a Coordinated System

California has a unique legislative mandate regarding children and youth involved in both the child welfare and juvenile justice systems. State law prohibits the simultaneous jurisdiction of the dependency and delinquency courts. The county probation department and the county welfare department are required to develop a written protocol to ensure a coordinated written assessment of any child involved in both the child welfare and the juvenile justice systems. The assessment must recommend either delinquent or dependent status for the child and the services the child should receive. A court, however, may order that a child be placed under dual supervision and receive services from both systems.

California statutes also contain a "joinder" law, whereby the juvenile or family court is granted the authority to manage youths' needs across agencies. The California law, referred to as §362, which was enacted in 1976 and amended to include reference to private-sector providers in 2003, allows a juvenile court, in an ongoing dependency proceeding, to "join" any agency or private service provider that owes an unmet duty to a child. In this situation, the judge acts as a manager and enforces agencies' responsibilities for the youth. This crossover case management effort has as its goal the facilitation of services across agency boundaries.

Working within California's legislative structure, Los Angeles County developed three processes to alert the child welfare or juvenile justice agency when a child becomes involved with the other agency. First, a juvenile automated index provides information about the dependency or delinquency status of any minor who comes into contact with either agency through detention, a filing by the Department of Child and Family Services (DCFS), or probation. The court receives this information at the first hearing and orders a joint assessment of the child. Second, the delinquency court calendar notes whether a child currently has or has had a case with DCFS. Third, the dependency court prints and posts in each courtroom a weekly report of all minor dependents of the court who have had contact with law enforcement in the week prior.

Kansas City, Missouri: KidSafe

The KidSafe program in Kansas City, Missouri, is one of five sites[4] OJJDP funded to reduce juvenile delinquency through the prevention of child abuse and neglect. OJJDP encourages each site to create its own approach to system reform. In the KidSafe program, the same court hears both the child welfare and delinquency cases, and the same judge is assigned to both cases. Youth are assigned a GAL and an attorney. The court makes a single disposition for the child, and although the judge may order joint agency custody and supervision, he or she usually specifies a lead agency. Professionals from one system are encouraged to access the services offered by the other system. In addition, workers can obtain information regarding the child's history with the child welfare or juvenile justice system from a computer system, which holds a "social file" on each child involved with either system. The KidSafe program began in Kansas City in 1998 and continues to operate today.

Michigan: The Juvenile Justice Online Technology (JJOLT) System

Michigan met the requirements of the reauthorized JJDPA by implementing a Web-based case management information system (MIS), specifically using the JJOLT system. This system is coordinated with the Service Worker Support System, which holds the data required by the federal child welfare reporting system, the Adoption and Foster Care Analysis and Reporting System.[5] The Service Worker Support System and JJOLT are able to share data. The Michigan MIS has a number of features. When a child comes into contact with the family court, which has jurisdiction over abused and neglected children and delinquent youth, a juvenile justice services caseworker completes an assessment in JJOLT. He or she then sends the case electronically to the Juvenile Justice Assignment Unit. JJOLT automatically searches for service providers based on the results of the assessment. An assignment specialist reviews the matches and current vacancies in the selected programs. Through this process, the system expedites assessment of the youth and provides the most appropriate services and placement. JJOLT operates statewide and meets the privacy and security requirements of the Health Insurance Portability and Accountability Act.

Summary of Coordination Efforts

Where programs developed to respond to youth dually involved in the child welfare and juvenile justice systems exist, their focus has been on information sharing and connecting youth with service providers that can offer the most appropriate and comprehensive assistance based on a complete and accurate assessment of the youth's and family's needs.

Agencies have used a number of innovative strategies to enhance juvenile justice and child welfare system coordination, and we can learn much from these efforts. As of yet, however, no truly comprehensive program model links the juvenile justice and child welfare systems when youth currently in foster care are arrested and brought before the juvenile court on delinquency petitions.

Changes in Federal Law that Promote Programs to Strengthen Collaboration

Recent changes in federal law reflect the federal government's interest in supporting more coordinated responses to youth who are involved in both the child welfare and juvenile justice systems. Congress amended two federal laws, JJDPA and the Child Abuse Prevention and Treatment Act (CAPTA), to address the multisystem needs of this group of youth. Both laws provide opportunities for the development of programs to strengthen the collaboration between the child welfare and juvenile justice systems.

- **Reauthorization of JJDPA.** On November 2, 2002, the President signed P.L. 107-273 reauthorizing JJDPA. Three specific provisions in the new law bridge the juvenile justice and child welfare systems. The legislation:

  - requires states, to the maximum extent possible, to establish policies and systems to incorporate relevant child protective services records into juvenile justice records for purposes of establishing and implementing treatment plans for juvenile offenders;

  - calls on states to ensure that juvenile offenders whose placements are funded using federal funds through Title IV-E foster care receive all the protections included in the foster care system; and

  - stipulates that within a year of enactment, a study will be conducted of "juveniles who were under the care or custody of the child welfare system or who are unable to return to their family after completing their disposition in the juvenile justice system" (42 USC §5661[a][4]). The study is to include an examination of the extent to which state juvenile justice systems and child welfare systems are coordinating services and treatment, and identification of the federal and local sources of funds used for placements and services and the barriers states face in providing services to these juveniles.[6]

In addition, the reauthorized JJDPA expands the categories of individuals whom states may serve through federal funding for juvenile delinquency prevention and treatment services to include victims of child maltreatment and children known to the child welfare system.

- **Reauthorization of CAPTA.** On June 25, 2003, the President signed the Keeping Children and Families Safe Act (P.L. 108-36) reauthorizing CAPTA. The law authorizes funding for CAPTA state and discretionary grants and research through FY 2008, including $120 million authorized for FY 2004. Current funding for CAPTA state grants is $22 million; discretionary grants, used for research and practice, are funded at $34 million. The legislation:

  - broadens the use of CAPTA state grants to include collaboration between child protective services and the juvenile justice system. Specifically, the amendments provide that CAPTA state grants may be used for "supporting and enhancing interagency collaboration between the child protection system and the juvenile justice system for improved delivery of services and treatment, including methods for continuity of treatment plan and services as children transition between systems";

  - expands the list of research activities that can be funded by the U.S. Department of Health and Human Services (DHHS) to include effective approaches for collaboration between child protective services and the juvenile justice system; and

  - requires states to submit a variety of new reports to DHHS on an annual basis. One report would provide for data collection regarding dually involved children. Specifically, the amendments state:

    Each State must work with the Secretary to provide, to the maximum extent practicable, a data report that includes the number of children under the care of the State child protection system who are transferred into the custody of the State juvenile justice system (42 USC §5106[d][14]).

Current Law

The third component of this study addressed the extent to which current law mandates that significant adults in the lives of youth receive notice and are given an opportunity to be heard in delinquency proceedings when a youth who is in foster care is arrested and charged with a delinquent act. Notice of delinquency proceedings allows caregivers to participate as advocates on behalf of youth in foster care who must appear before the court on delinquency charges. Research indicates that youth's caregivers may or may not receive notification of the youth's arrest, detention, and subsequent delinquency proceedings.

The authors conducted legal research to determine the extent to which the law requires notification of child welfare agencies and foster parents when youth in foster care are arrested, brought to a juvenile detention or intake facility, and brought before the juvenile court on delinquency petitions. First, they analyzed the extent to which the notice provisions in ASFA may provide for notice of juvenile delinquency hearings. Next, they conducted legal research into the statutes of 16 states[7] and the District of Columbia to determine the extent to which state law directs such notification to child welfare agencies or foster parents.

ASFA

ASFA provides little guidance on the rights of foster parents and child welfare agencies regarding notice of delinquency proceedings involving children in their care. ASFA, signed into law in 1997, amended Titles IV-B and IV-E of the Social Security Act and mandated that safety and permanence be the primary focus of child welfare practice. Under ASFA, the courts must give foster parents (including preadoptive parents) and relative caregivers notice and an opportunity to be heard at any hearing or review concerning a child in their care. The U.S. Children's Bureau has interpreted the ASFA notice requirements as applying to 12-month permanency hearings and 6-month review hearings. States, however, may require notice of additional child welfare proceedings.

Analysis suggests that the applicability of the ASFA notice requirements depends on the child's circumstances. It is likely that ASFA requirements of notice to foster parents and other caregivers apply if a court directs a Title IV-E eligible child to enter foster care as a result of a delinquency offense. If, however, a youth who is already in a foster care placement commits a delinquency offense, it appears that ASFA notice requirements would not apply to the delinquency proceeding. In the context of this study, which focuses on the latter situation, ASFA appears to offer little in the way of caregiver notice requirements, making state law all the more important on this issue.

State Statutory Provisions and Practice

The laws of all states now provide foster parents and child welfare agencies with statutory rights to notice and an opportunity to be heard in child welfare proceedings concerning children in their care. The rights of caregivers in juvenile delinquency proceedings, however, are less clear under states' laws. This study's research revealed a wide range of approaches to the individuals who must be given notice of a youth's delinquency proceedings. The key general findings were the following:

- Several states have statutes that acknowledge the right of the child's "parent, guardian, or custodian" to receive notice of and participate in delinquency hearings.[8] For children in foster care, these provisions require notice to the child welfare agency that holds custody of the youth. These statutes, however, do not specify that notice be given to the child's caseworker or foster parents, leaving the decision regarding notice to these individuals to agency policy and practice.

- Only a small number of state statutes provide notice rights to foster parents. Most states make no explicit mention of foster parents. Yet in some states' statutes, there are references to "custodian" or "person having physical custody of the child," provisions that could be interpreted to include foster parents.[9] In addition, several states provide that notice be given to "any person with whom the juvenile resides," a provision that also conceivably could extend to foster parents.[10]

- In addition to providing notice of delinquency proceedings to a youth's parent, guardian, or custodian, some states statutorily mandate the presence of these individuals at proceedings[11] and give the court authority to hold these individuals in contempt of court if they fail to appear.[12]

- Statutes in a number of states hold parents, guardians, or custodians accountable to varying degrees for crimes committed by youth in their care, including some statutes that hold these individuals financially liable for the care of the youth, order the payment of restitution, or require these adults to participate in counseling or other treatment programs.[13] Several states specifically exempt foster parents from accountability, whereas others specify that foster parents may be required to participate in court-ordered programs.[14]

As a result of their research, the authors identified states with statutes that seemed to best support good practice through provisions requiring notification of foster parents or child welfare caseworkers when youth in care are charged with delinquent acts—Alaska, Arkansas, Illinois, Ohio, and Minnesota. They contacted individuals in those ʰtates to learn whether agencies were implementing these promising statutes and whether they resulted in the actual involvement of these adults. The authors also contacted individuals in Kentucky, Texas, and Vermont—states not identified as having particularly strong statutes—to gather information about actual practice in those states. The results of the research suggested that in general, little connection exists between statutory requirements that foster parents or guardians receive notice of proceedings and actual practice, although there appeared to be a congruence between statutory requirements and practice in Alaska. The individuals in each state who were interviewed indicated that practice varies considerably by county. They typically were able to describe practice only in their own county. Interviews also revealed that most often, notice to caseworkers and foster parents occurred informally and without an awareness of statutory requirements.

The following provides more specific information regarding practices in the eight states in which the researchers conducted interviews.

Alaska

Alaska grants foster parents an explicit right to receive notice of and participate in juvenile proceedings involving children under their care.[15] The Alaska Department of Health and Social Services is statutorily responsible for providing notice of proceedings. According to the statute, when a police officer initially detains a minor, he or she must make reasonable efforts to give notice of the detention to the minor's parent or guardian, foster parent, and the Department of Health and Social Services.[16] At the detention hearing, the court must give the foster parent an opportunity to be heard.[17] According to an interviewee in Anchorage, Alaska is very successful in fulfilling this statutory mandate for the approximately 50 children who are involved in both the child welfare and juvenile justice systems at any one time.

Since 1989, Alaska's juvenile justice system and child welfare system have maintained a statewide database for all children involved in either system. Juvenile justice personnel can change or update only the data pertaining to a child's juvenile justice record, and child welfare workers can change or update only the data pertaining to a child welfare case. Both agencies, however, can view information that the other agency has entered. The juvenile justice and child welfare departments have entered into a memorandum of agreement with various entities that wish to have access to the database, including police departments, schools, and public assistance programs. The memorandum of agreement requires database users to keep information confidential and use it only for designated purposes. An interviewee in Alaska noted that despite concerns about privacy and confidentiality, child-serving agencies attempt to coordinate services and address children's needs in a comprehensive manner.

When police detain a youth in Alaska, the officer contacts a youth counselor from the juvenile justice division and an intake probation officer. The intake probation officer searches the shared database to determine whether the child has had any prior child welfare or juvenile court involvement and then contacts the child's birthparents and foster parents to inform them of the detention. The youth counselor also contacts and works with both the birthparents and foster parents.

An interviewee in Anchorage stated definitively that 100% of foster parents in Alaska are invited to participate in delinquency hearings for children under their care and that approximately 75% to 80% of foster parents exercise their right to participate in the hearings. In general, foster parents are considered to be parties to the case and are encouraged to participate in court proceedings. Agencies give foster parents copies of all court orders. The interviewee noted that when a foster parent's recommendation and a probation officer's assessment conflict, the court often follows the foster parent's recommendation.

Arkansas

The Arkansas code specifically provides that the Department of Human Services give notice to foster parents of "any review or hearing" held with respect to a child in their care and provide an opportunity for foster parents to be heard.[18] This section of the Arkansas code addresses both dependency and delinquency proceedings and does not specify whether notice must be provided to foster parents in child welfare hearings, delinquency proceedings, or both types of proceedings. Other sections of the Arkansas code specifically dealing with juvenile delinquency matters include no specific provision for notice or participation with respect to foster parents. Notice of a juvenile's arrest and notice of a detention hearing must be provided only to the child's "parent, guardian or custodian."[19] Although it appears that a public child welfare agency would qualify as such, it is unclear whether a foster parent would qualify. It is also unclear whether foster parents would fall within the scope of another section of the Arkansas code pertaining to delinquency that provides that "any person having care and control" of the juvenile shall be served with a copy of the charges and either a notice of the hearing or an order to appear.[20]

An interviewee in Arkansas stated that the system does not work very well with respect to children who are in foster care and are charged with delinquent acts. This individual indicated that the problem is not one of notice or the right to be heard but, instead, lies in the struggle to ensure that foster parents attend court proceedings. The interviewee commented that she rarely sees foster parents in court. She believed that foster parents frequently do not wish to deal with a child's legal problems and do not see attendance at court proceedings as their responsibility. She further noted that therapeutic foster care parents are much more likely to appear in court than foster parents who have not received specialized training.

This interviewee also stated that foster parents usually become aware of a youth's arrest fairly quickly because the child does not return home or the police officer or detention center contacts the foster parent. Typically, the police officer or detention center does not notify the caseworker at the time of the child's arrest. At the first court hearing, a search is conducted to determine whether any pending cases concern the child, including dependency cases. The interviewee felt that this system works because of the small number of courts in the county in which she works and the fact that all cases with respect to a child are assigned to the same court. If a pending child welfare case is identified in the first court hearing, the court notifies the caseworker at that time. The interviewee stated that generally, caseworkers do not believe it is their responsibility to appear in court for the initial hearing and do not do so, although they may appear at later proceedings.

This individual further reported that often no adult appears with a youth at the first hearing, which then results in the youth being detained. Moreover, the absence of a responsible adult at the detention hearing may affect disposition, as a judge may be more likely to commit a youth to the Department of Youth Services if there is no responsible and involved parent or other adult present.

Illinois

Two statutes in Illinois govern foster parents' notice of and participation in juvenile proceedings. The Foster Parent Law[21] states that foster parents have the right to be notified of all court hearings and the right to intervene in court proceedings. The Juvenile Court Act covers both child welfare and delinquency proceedings and specifies that notice of proceedings "shall be directed to the minor's parent, guardian or legal custodian."[22] The act explicitly gives foster parents and the agency designated as custodian of the minor the right to notice of proceedings brought under the act if the minor is dependent, abused, or neglected. In addition, the act gives foster parents the right to be heard by the court.

An interviewee in Illinois stated that when the police detain a child, they ask the child to identify his or her parents. If the youth mentions foster parents, they are notified of the child's detention. If no parent or guardian claims the child at the police station, the police begin probation screening. They contact the delinquency division of the public defender's office, which conducts a database search to determine the child's probation status and determines whether the youth is in foster care. If the youth is in foster care, the police notify the foster parents at that time, if they have not previously been notified. They also notify the public child welfare system and ask child welfare to send a representative to the police station. In addition, a supervisor of the Cook County public defender's office receives a weekly list of all youth who are involved in both delinquency and foster care proceedings. An interviewee stated that foster parents in Illinois have rights identical to birthparents in court proceedings. She reported that a delinquency case in Illinois does not go forward unless a birthparent or foster parent is present.

Another interviewee reported that the public child welfare system, the public guardian's office, and the probation office of the juvenile courts are well coordinated and that communication among the offices is quite good. She reported that in four years with the public child welfare system, she has never heard a foster parent complain that he or she failed to receive notice of a hearing or wished to participate in a hearing and was denied that right.

Ohio

Ohio law explicitly gives foster parents a right to receive notice of and participate in juvenile court proceedings, including delinquency proceedings, involving children under their care.[23] Opinions differ on the effectiveness of the law. One interviewee stated that the law, which went into effect in 1999, has increased foster parent participation in juvenile court proceedings, and that, in turn, has improved outcomes for children in foster care who commit delinquency offenses. Another interviewee, however, stated that the law has had little effect on the day-to-day operations of the court and that foster parents rarely attend or participate in juvenile proceedings. The interviewee said that the public child welfare agency discourages foster parents from participating and that the court system does not value their participation.

Ohio relies on youth to self-report their foster care status to police when they are detained. If a youth reports that he or she is in foster care, the police contact the foster parents. If a youth fails to self-report, the court generally discovers the youth's foster care status at the time of the first court appearance. In counties that use a one family–one judge assignment, the court that hears a delinquency matter routinely conducts a record search, and if the child is in foster care, obtains the child's welfare file and notifies the public child welfare agency. Responsibility for notifying the foster parents falls on the public child welfare agency.

One interviewee noted that the foster parent's right to participate is not well defined, although it also was reported that judges allow foster parents to submit written statements to the court. One individual, however, stated that foster parents typically have little to contribute to the adjudicatory phase. This interviewee stated that foster parent participation should be limited to the dispositional phase, when their knowledge of the youth's current behavior and progress is most relevant.

Another interviewee noted that she has never heard a foster parent complain about not receiving notice of delinquency proceedings. One interviewee informally surveyed foster parents who had experience with the delinquency court system. All surveyed families reported that the probation department or the police department notified them when the youth was detained, they felt welcome in the courtroom, and in most instances, the court solicited their input during the proceedings.

Minnesota

In Minnesota, rights to notice and participation in juvenile court proceedings are given to the youth's parent, guardian, or custodian, or "other persons having custody and control of the child."[24] Minnesota differs from other states with similar statutory language in that the law specifically mentions foster parents, which allows the court, in making a disposition, to consider any report or recommendation made by a number of individuals, including foster parents.[25]

Generally, individuals who were interviewed in Minnesota reported that notification of foster parents tends to happen informally but seems to be working. Interviewees in Olmstead and Ramsey Counties stated that notification goes to the address reported by the youth, and foster parents receive notification if the child lives with them. Representatives of local foster parent associations reported that social workers usually are the parties who provide information to foster parents about delinquency proceedings. An interviewee noted that in two years, she has not heard a foster parent complain about failure to receive notice of delinquency proceedings.

Texas

Under Texas law, most rights associated with delinquency proceedings extend to parents, guardians, or custodians, without reference to foster parents.[26] Statute defines *custodian* as the adult with whom the child resides. It is unclear from this statutory language whether foster parents have a right to notice of proceedings or a right to participate. Interviews with individuals in Travis County revealed that a youth is taken through an intake procedure after detention by police. The police ask the youth if he or she is in foster care or under the custody of child protective services. They send notification to whomever the child reports as the person with whom he or she is living, and as a result, notice to foster parents typically depends on youths' self-reports. In cases in which the police officer contacts the person identified by the youth and determines that the individual is not, in fact, the youth's actual guardian, the officer may make efforts to locate the child's foster family.

The Travis County interviewee stated that in smaller communities, law enforcement officials usually are familiar with the community and the protective services staff and are likely to easily determine that a youth is in foster care. When police determine that a youth is in the custody of child protective services, they contact protective services. In Travis County, a protective services worker always attends and participates in any hearing for the youth. One interviewee noted that foster parents have an opportunity to participate but often choose not to do so. In the interviewee's opinion, foster parents often are unable to attend proceedings due to work obligations.

Kentucky

Kentucky does not provide foster parents with a statutory right to receive notice of or an opportunity to participate in juvenile delinquency hearings. Workers generally give notice to the person having custody or control of the child, but it is not clear whether courts give foster parents or guardians an opportunity to participate in proceedings. Interviewees were unable to identify any procedures—formal or informal—for providing notice to foster parents or child welfare caseworkers. Interviewees in Kentucky also stated that the state does not have a coordinated computer system that can be used to determine which children are involved in the child welfare and juvenile justice systems.

Vermont

Vermont does not specifically provide foster parents with a statutory right to receive notice of and participate in juvenile justice hearings. Instead, the law generally only requires notice and an opportunity to participate for parents, guardians, or custodians, or in some cases, "a person having the child under his supervision."[27] In determining a disposition of a youthful offender, the court "shall obtain input from the child's parents, custodians or guardians, teachers, treatment providers, clergy, and all other persons that the court deems necessary."[28] Interviewees in Vermont indicated that staff encourage foster parents to be involved in delinquency proceedings and to bring the child to court if the child has not been detained. Interviewees commented that in most cases, foster parents become involved in the proceedings or they decide to end the child's placement with their family.

In Vermont, one administrative agency has responsibility for all Child in Need of Care or Supervision cases, including abuse and neglect, abandonment and foster care, and delinquency cases. The agency also operates and manages juvenile detention centers. One interviewee commented that because foster care and juvenile delinquency are the responsibility of the same department and only a small number of youth in the state are involved in both systems, the two areas work together seamlessly and notice of proceedings occurs easily. When the police arrest a youth in foster care, they inform the public child welfare agency, which then may ask the foster parents to be involved in the proceedings. An interviewee commented that social workers always attend delinquency proceedings with the youth. Moreover, the juvenile court regularly sends a list of juvenile justice cases to child welfare social workers. Interviewees in Vermont stated that the combination of social services and juvenile justice in one department is very positive. One particular benefit is that the social worker assigned to a child in foster care also serves as that child's probation officer.

Summary of State Laws Regarding Delinquency Proceedings

Despite the fact that foster parents and group home staff are likely to have information which would be useful to the delinquency court with jurisdiction over a youth who is in foster care, most states do not have a formal mechanism or statutory framework for providing these individuals with notice of proceedings and an opportunity to be heard by the court. In some cases, informal means of communication and local practice appear to adequately ensure that these individuals receive notice of proceedings. Law and practice, however, in most instances, do not recognize the insight that foster parents, caseworkers, and group home staff could provide to the court.

PART III

Recommendations

As more is understood about the experiences of and outcomes for youth involved in both the child welfare and juvenile justice systems, it is evident that significant efforts are needed to prevent children in the foster care system from entering the juvenile justice system. Efforts are needed to ensure that youth in foster care are well served by foster families who care for them; receive the mental health, educational, and other services they need; and have safe, permanent families, whether through reunification, long-term placement with relatives, or adoption. This report focuses on youth in foster care whose stays in care, often already troubled, have been made more complex by the fact that they commit delinquent acts while in care. The study's findings demonstrate that for many youth, it is the foster care system itself that precipitates their involvement in the juvenile justice system. Once they enter this system, it is clear that they face numerous obstacles. Some of the issues that this study identifies are many adults' perceptions of youth in foster care as future criminals, the likelihood that youth in care will appear in court without an adult to advocate for them (other than a lawyer), and the lack of communication and collaboration between the child welfare and juvenile justice systems when a youth is involved in both systems. Based on the findings of this report, the following recommendations are offered to help promote the best outcomes for these youth.

1. **Police departments and delinquency court officials in a jurisdiction should develop a system to identify detained youth who are in the custody of the child welfare system.** The timely identification of youth in foster care is imperative to ensure that adults responsible for the youth are notified of the youth's arrest, detention, and court proceedings. A number of jurisdictions across the country have implemented automated computer information systems or other systems that allow court officials to identify youth with current child welfare cases. Some jurisdictions rely on the operation of one family–one judge courtrooms to identify such youth. Law enforcement agencies and courts that currently do not have a timely, reliable method of identifying youths' child welfare involvement should make this a priority.

2. **Foster parents and group home staff should receive training and support so they can intervene effectively with youth and avoid police involvement unless absolutely necessary.** Numerous individuals interviewed for this study reported that the staff of group homes—and some foster parents—contact the police as a first resort when youth in care engage in troubling behaviors, relying on the police as the means of controlling the youth. Although in some situations it may be necessary to alert law enforcement, group home staff and foster parents should be able to respond effectively to youth in most situations. Foster parents should have access to training and support services so they do not feel the need to rely on police involvement on a routine basis. Group home staff likewise should receive training and supervisory support to effectively manage the group home environment. Group homes should have written protocols that clarify the circumstances in which police involvement is appropriate.

3. **Notice of delinquency proceedings should automatically extend to the adults who are legally responsible for the youth.** Those adults should be required parties to delinquency proceedings and should be informed about their responsibilities regarding the youth. In addition to the youth's attorney, individuals with legal custody of the youth should receive notification of all delinquency court proceedings (in writing, when time permits) and should be made required parties to the case. For

youth in foster care, the public child welfare agency is most often the legal custodian, and legal proceedings against a youth should not proceed until a representative of the child welfare agency is present.

4. **In addition to mandating the attendance of adults who have a legal obligation to attend delinquency proceedings, the delinquency court should ensure that adults who are familiar with the youth are invited to court proceedings and should solicit information from them.** The presence of a representative of the public child welfare agency and the youth's attorney in court will not ensure that an adult is present who can provide the court with insight about the youth. Other adults who are important figures in a youth's life, particularly foster parents, group home staff who are familiar with the youth, and a youth's GAL or CASA, should be encouraged to attend delinquency proceedings. These individuals should receive notice of the proceedings, be encouraged to attend, and be afforded an opportunity to provide the court with information about the youth at the dispositional phase of court proceedings. The value of adults who are dedicated to the youth appearing in court on his or her behalf cannot be overstated.

5. **A corps of attorneys who have a knowledge base in both child welfare law and juvenile delinquency law should be available to this group of youth.** Too often, youth are represented in delinquency court by attorneys who lack sufficient familiarity with the child welfare system. To ensure that youth who are currently in foster care receive legal representation that is responsive to all the youth's needs, youth should be represented by attorneys who have training in both juvenile delinquency law and child welfare law.

6. **Child welfare and juvenile justice systems should increase communication and collaboration across the two systems, taking advantage of available federal funding.** Although some jurisdictions have made great progress in fostering communication and collaboration between the child welfare and juvenile justice systems, much work remains in most communities across the country. Agencies can enhance intersystem communication

through the creation of a position designed to facilitate communication or the designation of such responsibility to an existing staff member, multisystem meetings, and cross-trainings of the various professionals who have some level of responsibility for a dually involved child, including judges, probation officers, child welfare administrators, supervisors, caseworkers, GALs, and CASAs. Furthermore, policies must clarify the roles and responsibilities of the numerous professionals who have a degree of responsibility for a dually involved youth. Several jurisdictions have had positive experiences with interagency MOUs that specify the roles of the systems regarding this class of youth. Delineation of responsibilities for a youth who is involved in both systems—including written guidelines outlining the roles and responsibilities of probation officers and child welfare caseworkers at various stages of court proceedings—is necessary to ensure an appropriate response to youth and to ensure accountability for this response. To the maximum extent possible, states should pursue funding opportunities for system coordination available through the reauthorized CAPTA and JJDPA laws.

7. **Agencies should conduct interdisciplinary training to ensure a unified, coherent response to youth who are involved in both the child welfare and juvenile justice systems.** Interdisciplinary training of judges, attorneys, probation personnel, detention personnel, child welfare professionals, law enforcement, foster parents, and volunteers such as GALs and CASAs should be conducted with the goal of more effectively responding to youth involved in both the child welfare and juvenile justice systems. In addition to addressing the roles and responsibilities of the individuals involved with the youth, this training should address child development, separation and loss, bonding and attachment, the effects of substance abuse on behavior, and strategies for meeting the medical, mental health, educational, and vocational needs of youth. Many of these individuals also would benefit from training concerning the application of the ASFA to dependency and delinquency cases, particularly as the provisions affect procedural requirements and Title IV-E funding eligibility.

Conclusion

This report focuses on the experiences of young people in foster care who become involved with the juvenile justice system as a result of a delinquent act. It provides findings from qualitative research using interviews with child welfare and juvenile justice professionals, judges, foster parents, child welfare administrators, and, importantly, young adults who were living in foster care when arrested for delinquent acts. This report identifies existing programs that respond to the needs of youth involved in the two systems and provides the results of legal research into state law to determine the extent to which the law requires notification of child welfare agencies and foster parents when youth in foster care appear before the delinquency court. The findings in each of these areas highlight the key issues that we must address to ensure that the juvenile justice system treats youth in foster care equitably and justly and that these youth receive the services and placements that appropriately meet their needs from both the juvenile justice and child welfare systems. Judges, probation officers, attorneys, child welfare caseworkers, administrators of child welfare and juvenile justice systems, group home staff, and foster parents can do much to ensure that any disadvantages these youth face before the delinquency court are minimized and that youth are provided with coordinated services which are responsive to their needs.

References

Armstrong, M. L. (1998). *Adolescent pathways: Exploring the intersection between child welfare and juvenile justice, PINS and mental health.* New York: Vera Institute of Justice.

Child Welfare League of America. (2002). *Raising the level of awareness between child maltreatment and juvenile delinquency: Results of an on-line survey.* Washington, DC: Author. Retrieved December 3, 2003, from http://www.cwla.org/programs/juvenilejustice/jjdsurvey.htm.

Conger, D., & Ross, T. (2001). *Reducing the foster care bias in juvenile detention decisions: The impact of Project Confirm.* New York: Vera Institute of Justice.

Davies, H. J., & Davidson, H. A. (2001). *Parental involvement practices of juvenile courts.* Washington, DC: American Bar Association Center on Children and the Law.

Deihl, R. M., Martin, M., & Nunez, S. (2002). *Caregivers and the courts: Improving court decisions affecting children in foster care.* Oakland, CA: National Center for Youth Law.

English, D. J., Widom, C. S., & Brandford, C. (2001). *Childhood victimization and delinquency, adult criminality, and violent criminal behavior: A replication and extension.* Washington, DC: U.S. Department of Justice, National Institute of Justice.

Jonson-Reid, M., & Barth, R. (2000). From placement to prison: The path to adolescent incarceration from child welfare supervised foster or group care. *Children and Youth Services Review, 22*, 493–516.

Jonson-Reid, M., & Barth, R. P. (2003). Probation foster care as an outcome for children exiting child welfare foster care. *Social Work, 48*, 348–361.

Maxfield, M. G., & Widom, C. S. (1996). The cycle of violence: Revisited six years later. *Archives of Pediatrics and Adolescent Medicine, 150,* 390–395.

Pawaserat, J. (1991). *Identifying Milwaukee youth in critical need of intervention: Lessons from the past, measures for the future.* Milwaukee, WI: University of Wisconsin Employment and Training Institute.

Runyan, D. K., & Gould, C. L. (1985). Foster care for child maltreatment: Impact on delinquent behavior. *Pediatrics, 75,* 562–568.

Ryan, J. P., & Testa, M. F. (2004). *Child maltreatment and juvenile delinquency: Investigating the role of placement and placement instability.* Urbana-Champaign, IL: Children and Family Research Center, School of Social Work, University of Illinois at Urbana-Champaign.

Slavin, P. (2001). From child maltreatment to delinquency. *Children's Voice, 10*(2), 24–25, 28–30.

Smith, C., & Thornberry, T. P. (1995). The relationship between childhood maltreatment and adolescent involvement in delinquency. *Criminology, 33,* 451–477.

Widom, C. S. (1989). The cycle of violence. *Science, 244,* 160–166.

Widom, C. S. (1992). *The cycle of violence* (Research in brief). Washington, DC: U.S. Department of Justice, National Institute of Justice.

Wiig, J., Widom, C. S., & Tuell, J. A. (2003). *Understanding child maltreatment and juvenile delinquency: From research to effective program, practice, and systemic solutions.* Washington, DC: Child Welfare League of America.

Additional Resources

Armstrong, M. (2000). The importance of bridging the gap between child welfare and juvenile justice for arrested foster youth. *Practicing Law Institute: Criminal Law and Urban Problems, 185*, 55–76.

Bellinger, M. E. (2000). "Can we talk?" Facilitating communication between dependency and delinquency courts. *Journal of Juvenile Law, 21*, 1–24.

Child Welfare League of America. (2001a). The Iowa example: Decategorization and the comprehensive strategy process. *The Link: Connecting Juvenile Justice and Child Welfare, 1*(3), 2.

Child Welfare League of America. (2001b). The Kentucky experience: Serving youth from prevention to aftercare. *The Link: Connecting Juvenile Justice and Child Welfare, 1*(2), 1.

Child Welfare League of America. (2001c). Wraparound Milwaukee provides innovative approach to system of care. *The Link: Connecting Juvenile Justice and Child Welfare, 1*(1), 1.

Child Welfare League of America. (2003). Michigan's Juvenile Justice Online Technology: A system of care for child welfare and juvenile justice. *The Link: Connecting Juvenile Justice and Child Welfare, 2*(3), 1.

Hemrich, V. E. (1999). Applying ASFA to delinquency and status offender cases. *ABA Child Law Practice, 18*(9), 129–135.

Institute on Criminal Justice, University of Minnesota Law School. (1999). *Hennepin County Juvenile Assessment Center planning project.* Minneapolis, MN: University of Minnesota.

Kamradt, B. (2000). Wraparound Milwaukee: Aiding youth with mental health needs. *Juvenile Justice, 7*(1), 14–23.

Kelly, B. T., Thornberry, T. P., & Smith, C. A. (1997). *In the wake of child maltreatment* (OJJDP juvenile justice bulletin). Washington, DC: U.S. Office of Juvenile Justice and Delinquency Prevention.

Maxfield, M. G., & Widom, C. S. (2001). *An update on the cycle of violence* (Research in brief). Washington, DC: U.S. Department of Justice, National Institute of Justice.

Ross, T., Conger, D., & Armstrong, M. (2002). Bridging child welfare and juvenile justice: Preventing unnecessary detention of foster children. *Child Welfare, 81*, 471–494.

Weiss, C. P. (1999). Improving communication and coordination between the child welfare and juvenile justice systems. *ABA Child Law Practice, 18*(9), 141–148.

Wiebush, R., Freitag, R., & Baird, C. (2001). *Preventing delinquency through improved child protection services* (Juvenile justice bulletin). Washington, DC: U.S. Department of Justice.

Endnotes

1. This preliminary information was obtained from the National Center for Juvenile Justice (NCJJ) prior to the completion of their research in Arizona. NCJJ indicated it intended to obtain a more accurate and up-to-date count during a subsequent stage of the study. This study should be available in September 2004 on the NCJJ website at http://www.ncjj.org.

2. The researchers selected states with which they had geographical familiarity or professional contacts. The states were Alabama, Alaska, Arkansas, Connecticut, Illinois, Indiana, Iowa, Kentucky, Massachusetts, Minnesota, Nevada, New Jersey, New York, Ohio, Texas, and Vermont.

3. In New York City, case planning responsibility does not terminate as a result of a youth's arrest. Case planning responsibility ends only when approved by an Administration of Children's Services case manager. By law, foster care agencies must assume physical custody of any youth in their care if the youth is released by the juvenile justice system.

4. The other sites are Chittendon County, Vermont; Toledo, Ohio; Huntsville, Alabama; and the Sault Sainte Marie Tribe in Michigan.

5. The Adoption and Foster Care Analysis and Reporting System (AFCARS) collects case-level information on all children in foster care for whom state child welfare agencies have responsibility for placement, care, or supervision and on children who are adopted under the auspices of the state's public child welfare agency. States are required to submit AFCARS data semiannually to the U.S. Administration for Children and Families.

6. The Office of Juvenile Justice and Delinquency Prevention is in the preliminary planning process for this study, for which the government authorized no appropriations. A completion date has not been announced.

7. The states were Alabama, Alaska, Arkansas, Connecticut, Illinois, Indiana, Iowa, Kentucky, Massachusetts, Minnesota, Nevada, New Jersey, New York, Ohio, Texas, and Vermont.

8. See, e.g., Wash. Rev. Code § 13.40.050; Ind. Code § 31-37-12-2.

9. Or. Rev. Stat. §419C.303, 306 (requires person who has physical custody of child to appear in court with child); Utah Code Ann. §78-3a-110 (person who has physical custody of child obligated to attend, as well as parent or guardian).

10. Kan. Stat. Ann. §38-1626 (summons and copy of complaint served on person having legal custody, person with whom juvenile residing, and any other person designated by county or district attorney); N.H. Rev. Stat. Ann. §169-B:7 (person having custody of or living with the minor is summoned); N.Y. Fam. Code Ann. §12.2 (court to summon the juvenile and his or her parent or other person legally responsible for care, or if not available, then the person with whom the youth resides); D.C. Code Ann. §16-2325.1 (court can order person with whom child resides, other than parent or guardian, to be present at court proceedings).

11. Minn. Stat. §260B.163 (parent or guardian must accompany child at each hearing); Nev. Rev. Stat. §62.140 (person having custody of the child is summoned).

12. N.C. Gen. Stat. §7B-1805 (parent, guardian, or custodian is subject to finding of criminal contempt for failure to appear at a scheduled hearing).

13. Tenn. Code Ann. §37-1-174 (court may order parent or legal guardian to participate in child's treatment or rehabilitation and complete community service work individually or jointly with child).

14. Cal. Welf. & Inst. §729.5 (restitution cannot be imposed on foster parents); Ala. Code §6-5-271 (foster parent not liable for value of merchandise shoplifted by minor); Alaska Stat. §34.50.020 (state agency or foster parents not liable for property damages in tort); Cal. Welf. & Inst. §727 (court can require parent, guardian, or foster parent to participate in programs, counseling, or education); D.C. Code Ann. §16-2320 (if child found delinquent, court has jurisdiction over any parent or caregiver to secure his or her cooperation in the rehabilitation process).

15. Alaska Stat. §14.12.050(a) and §47.12.110.

16. Alaska Stat. §47.12.250(b).

17. Alaska Stat. §47.12.250(c).

18. Ark. Code Ann. §9-27-325(l); §9-27-325(1)(3)(a).

19. Ark. Code Ann. §9-27-313; §9-27-326.

20. Ark. Code Ann. §9-27-312.

21. IL ST Ch. 20 §520.

22. IL ST Ch. 705§405.

23. Ohio Rev. Code Ann. §2151.424(A).

24. Minn. Stat. §260B.151[3].

25. Minn. Stat. Ann. §260B.193.

26. Tex. Rev. Civ. Stat. Ann. §52.02(b)(1); §52.04(d); §54.01.

27. VT ST T.33§5519.

28. Vt ST T.33§5519[b].